REAL LIFE

IN

CASTRO'S

CUBA

REAL LIFE

IN

CASTRO'S

CUBA

CATHERINE MOSES

A Scholarly Resources Inc. Imprint
Wilmington, Delaware

© 2000 by Scholarly Resources Inc.
All rights reserved
First published 2000
Printed and bound in the United States of America

Scholarly Resources Inc.
104 Greenhill Avenue
Wilmington, DE 19805-1897
www.scholarly.com

Library of Congress Cataloging-in-Publication Data
Moses, Catherine, 1965–
    Real life in Castro's Cuba / Catherine Moses.
      p.   cm. — (Latin American silhouettes)
    Includes bibliographical references and index.
    ISBN 0-8420-2836-6 (cloth : alk. paper). — ISBN 0-8420-2837-4
(paper : alk. paper)
    1. Cuba—Description and travel.   2. Cuba—Social conditions—
1959–   3. Cuba—Economic conditions—1959–   4. Political
persecution—Cuba—History. I. Title. II. Series.
F1765.3.M68   1999
972.9106′4—dc21   99-24812
                                                    CIP

⊗ The paper used in this publication meets the minimum requirements of
the American National Standard for permanence of paper for printed library
materials, Z39.48, 1984.

About the Author

Catherine Moses is a former U.S. Foreign Service Officer. Before working in press and cultural affairs at the United States Interests Section in Havana, Cuba, she served in the American Embassy in Bogotá, Colombia, and in Beijing, China. She is a graduate of Rice University.

Contents

Acknowledgments xi

Introduction 1

PART I The Cuban Reality

1 Loyalty to the Revolution 7

2 *No Es Fácil:* Food and Daily Life 25

3 *Hay Que Resolver:* Working for Pesos and Dollars 35

4 Varadero: Life for Tourists 55

5 Triumphs of the Revolution: Health Care and Education 65

6 Civil Society 75

7 Why Don't They Rise Up? 81

8 Good Intentions 85

9 America! 93

10 Migration 99

11 The Migration Accords 105

12 News and Information 117

13 The Opposition, Concilio Cubano, and February 24 125

14 The Fifth Party Plenum: Requiem for Hope 137

15 Reminiscing 141

PART II The Cuban Spirit

16 *Soy Cuba:* I Am Cuba 145

17 Spirit and Soul 153

18 *Caridad del Cobre* 173

Index 177

Acknowledgments

Writing a book is a solitary action, but it cannot be done without the encouragement and help of others. Without my parents' support, I might not have been able to create this work. They gave me a place to write the first draft, they listened as I read each chapter aloud, and they gave me strength when I faced setbacks. My gratitude also goes to Lester Langley, who believed in this manuscript and helped me find a publisher. My thanks go as well to Franklin Knight and Stanley Fish, who gave me much needed professional encouragement.

Vick Fisher, who took the cover photograph, enriched this book with more than his art. He saved the letters I wrote to him during my stay in Havana, and he sent them to me when I began work on the book so that I could use them as a reference. Another individual to whom I owe a debt of gratitude is Robert Rhudy, who read the manuscript in detail and helped me refine it.

It was, however, the Cubans I know who made this book possible. For my dear and wonderful friends who are still on the island and to those who have come to America, I wish for you *mucho amor y muchas bendiciónes.*

Introduction

No hay mal que dura cien años ni cuerpo que lo resiste.
There is nothing bad that lasts a hundred years, nor is there
a body that can resist that long.—Cuban proverb

Sitting on the seawall of the Malecón gazing north from Havana, I knew that my country was ninety miles and almost forty years away. I longed for America. I missed the freedom, and I missed my family. I was living in a world where 1940s and 1950s Fords and Chevys shared the road with Soviet trucks and Chinese bicycles. Faded pastel buildings with crumbling facades whispered tales of a bygone era, and roosters crowed in the center of the city. It was a strange and sad world but passionate and compelling.

Now, back in America, my mind travels, and I long for Cuba. Even though I cannot claim a drop of Cuban blood, after twenty months of living on the island, Cuba is an indelible part of my soul. I arrived in Cuba in February 1995 to work as an American diplomat in Havana. Little did I know, when I stepped from the airplane that first time, how dramatically the struggles, the pain, and the faith of these people would be etched into the fabric of my being.

Cuba is as distant to me now as America once was, and I am not able to bridge the gap between these two worlds except through words. Although our governments are at odds, I love the Cuban people. They have been my friends, my neighbors, and my colleagues. I was blessed during the time I spent on the island because Cubans trusted me and shared their world with me, a world that few Americans ever see. I saw private tears, and I saw true joy. I watched people face fear, and I knew of their hope that one day things might change. They are a people who try to live with dignity. I wrote this book for the Cubans, but it was written by them as well. Their stories and the world that they revealed to me are the foundation of this book. Because of the nature of politics on the island, I have changed most names to obscure true identities.

Cuba exists in an alternate reality; it is another world from another time. Mostly cut off from the Western world for more than three decades, it has evolved along its own path. It has become a curious mixture of Spanish Caribbean, socialist ideals gone awry, memories of what was, and a desperate need to survive. The Cuba held in the memory of those who knew the island before the Revolution is virtually gone. All that remains are broad boulevards, once dramatic buildings, and a sapphire sea, which together provide the backdrop for the drama of Cuba today. The dream of a socialist utopia also has faded. It is real now for only a handful of revolutionaries and those who have too much to lose should the regime change. Above the entrance to the tunnel on Linea, a main thoroughfare, hangs a neon sign declaring "*Socialismo o Muerte*" (Socialism or death). The "e" at the end of *Muerte* dangles at a precarious angle. The image is an apt reflection of Fidel Castro's Revolution.

Havana, an elegant, graceful city, has been brought to its knees. The city suffers from more than a lack of paint. The architectural wealth is dissolving, as torrential tropical rains tear at weathered facades. Balconies lean on improvised scaffolding, and skeletons are all that remain of buildings that have collapsed under the weight of rain and time. The island's infrastructure, although supported for years by enormous Soviet subsidies, is disintegrating. Water pipes rupture, spouting water, and are not repaired. Electricity goes out for long periods without explanation. Transportation for most consists of squeezing onto a packed 300-passenger bus with no air-conditioning, standing precariously on the platform bed of a one and one-half-ton truck, hitchhiking, or paying precious hard currency for a ride halfway across town. But the grass at the Lenin Monument in Parque Lenin is mowed.

Cuba has many voices, and they are often contradictory. The nation is educated but starving for information, proud but prostituting its daughters, revolutionary but suffocating. The island faces a dearth of basic material necessities yet holds a treasure of spiritual wealth. Confronted with an unrelenting scarcity of food, fuel, clothing, and medicine, Cubans spend long hours obtaining the most basic goods. They have had to become tremendously creative with making do with what little they have. Bits of wire and string and carefully reworked cans are used by inventive mechanics to keep ancient cars running even though no parts are available. Inspired cooks make candy from banana peels.

In addition to the economic travails, the political situation allows no freedom of expression or association. Fidel Castro demands loyalty to his Revolution, and that loyalty requires an ideological rigidity with no deviance from the Party line. Education, one of the triumphs of his Revolution, has actually contributed to the tragedy on the island. While Fidel's guarantee of education has meant that the people have learned to read, write, and think, political restrictions create a fear that ties their hands and gags their mouths, so they can neither read about new ideas nor write or speak about their own. The minds of thinking people are held captive.

Despite the great adversity they face, or perhaps because of it, Cubans have turned to one another and to their faith to survive. There is a profound spirituality at the heart of being Cuban. Catholicism and mystical traditions blend with a deep will to live, endowing the people with a unique spirit. It is this spirit that brings young lovers to the Malecón, that moves an old woman to dance in a park in Santiago de Cuba, that inspires jazz musicians to new rhythms and melodies, that gives a priest the strength to call from his pulpit for political reform, and that moves Cubans to give love because there is nothing else to give.

Cubans have a greater humanity and concern for one another than most of us can imagine. In spite of all the sadness and the daily suffering, Cuba is terribly alive, pulsing with the activity and passion of life. On the streets, people talk and gossip with friends and neighbors, sharing pains and triumphs, while salsa music blares from radios. There is an energy on the streets, a sense of community. If you are seeing your neighbors, you are part of life. Whether Guajira music is sung around a piano with the legendary Celina Gonzalez improvising on "Guantanamera," or the rhythm of Changuito's drum moves you with its Afro-Cuban sound, there is a vibrant spirit to life. This is a rich and mad place.

When I left the island, I knew I had to tell the story of the world I had encountered. For most Americans, Cuba is hidden behind the overwhelming image of Fidel Castro. With this book, I hope to help lift the veil that conceals Cuba from Americans and offer a glimpse of the many human faces of the island. The paths of the United States and Cuba are entwined. If our two nations are one day to interact positively, Americans must begin to truly understand the Cuban present and the Cuban people.

PART I　The Cuban Reality

< I >

Loyalty to the Revolution

Socialismo o muerte. Patria o muerte. Venceremos!
(Socialism or death. Fatherland or death. We shall overcome!)
—closing to all of Fidel's speeches

Socialism or death? Why don't we all just die now
and get it over with?—an intellectual's response

Late one Sunday afternoon, Estella was watching television. When Fidel appeared on the screen, she began to clap her hands and cry "Viva Fidel!" Her brown eyes sparkled as she cooed, "He is so handsome! What a leader. Viva Fidel!" A few moments later she began to giggle and then started singing a children's ditty. Her son's boyfriend sat down in front of her and patiently began to feed her. Estella was seventy-six years old. Since a stroke two years before, she functioned with a young child's mind and could not care for herself. She spent her days sitting in a lawn-type rocking chair in the sun-dappled living room of her architect son's apartment. A tin bowl was kept beneath the chair because she could no longer control her bladder. Before her stroke, she had been stern, serious, and a staunch revolutionary. Now she laughs with innocence, occasionally blurts out sexual comments, and calls for someone to pay attention to her if she feels lonely. Yet despite the many changes in her mind and body, she still loves Fidel.

For the Cubans, he is "Fidel," not Castro as Americans usually call him. He is an intimate part of their lives. They might not like him, might complain about him, might see his failings, and might blame him for all the country's problems, but he is Fidel. He is in control of the island and will be for the foreseeable future. Cubans have no other option. He is the focus of all that is political. Fidel is the Revolution. He is the law, the government, the guiding figure. He is to be revered, honored, and feared. If there is an important decision to be made, he will make it, because he is the center of power. Loyalty to him is loyalty to the Revolution.

Fidel is a highly intelligent man with great charisma. When, for example, he arrived at the Mexican National Day celebration in September 1995, there was no need to announce his presence. Electricity seemed to course through the crowd as a semicircle five people deep turned to focus on him. Fidel, however, is now over seventy. Though he can still electrify an audience, his rhetoric has not fundamentally changed in over thirty-five years and his promises are ringing hollow. While most of the world has abandoned the socialist path he pursues, at this point he cannot change his ways, for doing so would be to admit he had taken the wrong path or had made poor decisions. In an interview with Bernard Shaw of Cable News Network (CNN) on October 22, 1995, Fidel said that what happens to Cuba after he dies is not his problem. He continued, "That is the problem for the ones who come after me." For the rest of his life, Fidel's sole interest is his own power.

When Fidel speaks, radio and television broadcast the entire speech and usually rerun it. Shortly thereafter, one of the newspapers prints the text. Newsprint is precious in Cuba, and all papers are controlled by the State. An entire issue of the Communist Party daily, *Granma,* would fit onto four pages of any major U.S. newspaper, so one of Fidel's speeches and the accompanying commentary can easily dominate most of an edition. When Fidel addresses the Cuban people, he speaks like a grandfather to young children. One evening I watched a televised address he gave at the University of Havana, which he began by describing his own education. In his trademark lengthy style of delivery, after more than an hour he had just reached his experiences of second grade. Deciding to take a break, I went outside. Strangely, my television seemed to be the only one on in the neighborhood. When the Saturday night movies and the evening news were on, there was always a chorus of televisions playing at high volume. Cubans told me that when Fidel comes on the screen, most people turn off the sound, but they leave the picture on so they know when he finishes and the evening soap opera begins.

Although Cubans may not want to watch Fidel for hours on television, they carefully read his speeches in the newspaper. Paying attention to what he says is a matter of political survival. When Fidel speaks about an event in a critical tone, the people know that those involved are in trouble. For instance, after the U.S. Interests Section, the American diplomatic mission in Cuba, sponsored a visit by a U.S. specialist in teaching English, Fidel complained that the Americans were now even sending English teachers to subvert the island. Cuban teachers of English, although in great demand, found themselves treading on thin political ice. On another occasion, after the 1996 Olympics, Fidel took on equestrian events, claiming that such an expensive sport was for rich people only and that no Latin American country had enough money to support an equestrian team. The faces at the horseback riding center at Parque Lenin were very long; the trainers, who are members of Cuba's national team, feared losing their jobs because Fidel had implied that the resources for riding should be redistributed to other areas. It does not matter if what he says is accurate. After reading one of his speeches in which he made blatant errors, I burst out, "How can he lie like this?" The quick response of a nearby Cuban was, simply, "He has been lying to us for years."

Fidel and his Revolution demand loyalty, but the loyalty of most Cubans is not as easily obtained as the childlike devotion of the elderly Estella. For that reason, there is a complex system in place that is designed to ensure the acquiescence of the people. The massive bureaucracy of the State is dedicated to carrying out the will of the Revolution. The State encompasses all aspects of life: health, education, journalism, economics, agriculture, and law. Even marriage is affected, with the civil ceremony referring to socialist love. There is an important link in Cuba, as there was in the former Soviet Union, between economic and political survival. The State is responsible for providing for all of life's basic needs, but it requires the loyalty and consent of the citizens to maintain its power. The people need housing, food, and health care, and they know the only way to obtain them under the system is to toe the line. The State provides these basic necessities, and the people provide their loyalty, even if that loyalty is superficial and merely the formality of going through the motions. In turn, Cubans never have to worry about house payments or college tuition costs. Although it may not be much food, or good food, there is food. By remaining participants in the system, Cubans retain the safety net of food, shelter, and health care. Dissenting or being seen as counterrevolutionary in any way can result in the loss of some or all privileges and may lead to imprisonment.

To monitor the loyalty of the nation's citizens, Fidel created an extensive, and presumably efficient, State Security apparatus. I say "presumably efficient" because the Cubans certainly believe that the State knows everything about them. If they buy or sell on the black market (which almost everyone does), they are convinced that the State will be aware of the transaction. They always assume that someone is listening to their conversations and informing on them. Since no one is sure who is an informant, people find it difficult to trust others in their community or at work. In neighborhoods throughout Cuba, the State-sponsored Committee for the Defense of the Revolution (CDR) keeps a close eye on comings and goings, noting whether someone is drinking too much, is having marital problems, is ill, is straying from the Revolution, or is having contact with foreigners. In addition to keeping tabs on everyone, the CDR has neighborhood clean-up programs and guarantees that people turn out to vote. If there is an activity that requires participation, the Committee knocks on the door of any individual who does not show up. In the workplace, as well, the Party faithful are present and watching, and recklessly spoken words or counterrevolutionary attitudes can cost a job and a livelihood. Because no one knows who is working for State Security, colleagues, in moments of anger, point fingers at one another, exchanging heated accusations of being an informant. There is a sense that one is never alone.

As a result of the State's vigilance, Cubans have developed hand gestures and other subtle communication techniques to express words that they cannot speak in a critical tone. The hand gesture for State Security, for example, is tapping the first two fingers of the hand on the opposite shoulder. The most common signal for Fidel is made by pulling the fingers and thumb down from the chin as if stroking an imaginary beard. Creativity in communication is not limited to hand gestures. The spoken language in Cuba is multilayered, since meanings must often be conveyed through carefully chosen words. Those who trust each other develop a cryptic, elliptical way of talking, which is referred to as "speaking Chinese." When one of my Cuban friends told someone that I speak Mandarin Chinese, the Cuban's response was, "So what? Everyone here speaks Chinese." Words take on different meanings, and references to Fidel are veiled behind such nicknames as "*El Caballo*" (the horse) and "*El Barbudo*" (the bearded one). At one point during the Special Period, a time of great economic hardship that began with the collapse of the Soviet Union, Fidel was referred to jokingly as "*NiNi*" (neither nor), meaning neither electricity, nor food, nor water, nor much of anything. Among groups of friends, ways of speaking emerge so that conversations may be had with some privacy. Being detained by State Security may be called "a scholarship," for example, because one could say, "My son received a scholarship," and no outsider would think that anything bad had happened. Conversations are guarded, and meanings have to be inferred.

I understand the need Cubans feel to guard their actions and their words, because foreigners and diplomats, too, are under the scrutiny of State Security. My house was bugged and watched. The Cubans who visited me were well aware of the surveillance. One friend came to my house wearing a scarf and sunglasses, traveling as incognito as she could on her bicycle. I doubt, however, that her effort disguised her from the prying eyes of the State. It seemed that wherever I went in Havana I was *muy bien acompañada* (well accompanied). In Spanish that phrase often implies that one has a charming male escort. In this case, my companions never spoke to me, but I recognized them, with their white Guayabera shirts, khaki pants, and well-groomed mustaches. Our eyes would meet, and there was an unspoken acknowledgment; they were watching. Whenever I visited a Cuban, I knew that if for some reason my keepers were not watching me, then the ever-vigilant local network of the CDR would report on my actions effectively, thus defending the neighborhood from any threat it thought I presented. On several occasions when I left the city of Havana, I was followed closely, even though I traveled in either American or Japanese cars that easily outpaced the normal versions of the Soviet-made Lada, a common car in Cuba. On trips to the beach or provincial towns, a car would appear behind me, usually a white or dark blue Lada. These cars must have had supercharged engines, for, remarkably, they could keep pace. The cars also had distinctive tall radio antennas, which I assume, let the drivers communicate with headquarters.

The State justifies much of this demand for absolute loyalty by pointing to the looming threat posed by the United States. The Revolution considers the United States to be the enemy. Around the world, the threat of an external enemy has been a significant factor in helping authoritarian regimes stay in power. The Bay of Pigs, referred to by the Cuban government as the Victory at Playa Giron—"the first triumph over imperialism in Latin America"—is celebrated annually. To defend itself from America, Cuba has a large standing army, compulsory military service, and tunnels in which civilians

can hide should there be an invasion. Television programs emphasize the achievements of the troops and the readiness of the island
for attack, as if American aircraft carriers were looming on the horizon. These precautions may be extreme. As one American diplomat
commented, "The only thing likely to invade Cuba is mosquitoes."
Still, the island receives mixed messages from the United States. Certain conservative American politicians continue to use fiery rhetoric and threats of military action against Cuba. In addition, the
maneuverings of some Miami-based groups, which range from conducting military-type training exercises to making threats on the life
of Fidel Castro, have given the State reason to question U.S. intentions. The Cuban government uses these perceived threats and in-
flammatory rhetoric to make a case for maintenance of the military
machine.

If the threat of impending invasion were not enough to rouse the
specter of the United States as the enemy, there is the U.S. embargo
of the island, an economic measure that has done little more to affect the Castro regime in thirty-five years than to give it a scapegoat.
The State refers to the U.S. embargo as the *bloqueo* (blockade), as if
the United States had ships surrounding the island. The regime
blames all of Cuba's economic ills on the embargo, even though most
problems are the result of socialist mismanagement. All over the island there are billboards that say in red, white, and blue—the colors of Cuba's flag—*Por la Vida, No al Bloqueo!* (For life, no to the
blockade!). Conversations about shortages often touch on the embargo, but many Cubans admit that the embargo is not to blame
for much of their troubles.

Americans are the imperialists, the *Yanki* invaders. The United
States is the home of what the Cuban press calls the "troglodyte"
Jesse Helms and the "mafiosos" of Miami. Cubans are constantly
warned that these "fascists" want to take over the island and destroy
the Revolution. As if to fully clarify the State's position, there is a
billboard facing the U.S. diplomatic mission in Havana that has a

cartoon of a threatening Uncle Sam on one bit of land, a cartoon of a heroic revolutionary on another bit of land, and the declaration, "Mr. Imperialist: We have absolutely no fear of you!"

Although it may be that the State has no fear of imperialism, anyone having contact with the U.S. Interests Section can suffer an untimely political death. The Cuban government is very much afraid of ideas from outside Cuba. If the wretched imperialists are not trying to undermine the regime through military force or the economic embargo, they are trying to undermine it with poisonous ideas of liberty. In that battle of ideas, many Cubans have been drawn into the line of fire. Academics, journalists, artists, and others with intellectual curiosity are attracted to the new and provocative ideas in American literature, scholarly work, magazines, and newspapers. Unfortunately, despite their allure, these materials are not only rare in Cuba but they are suspect and can be considered enemy propaganda. While it may be possible for the State to control the physical actions of the people, it has been increasingly difficult for the Revolution to retain intellectual loyalty. In a speech at the Fifth Party Plenum on March 23, 1996, Raul Castro, Fidel's younger brother, noted that tourists, foreign businessmen, and diplomats were potentially dangerous to Cuba because they bring foreign ideas.

Cubans fall politically into three categories: the Party faithful and true believers, those outside the system, and those within the system who no longer believe. The Party faithful are those who still believe in the Revolution and Fidel. They defend the system and present the Party line with fervor. Some of these followers are from classes that have benefited from the Revolution, and they see Fidel as a great hero and leader. Others have attained position and privilege by maintaining a dedication to the Party and the Revolution. Since they have a great deal to lose if Fidel falls, they are likely to do all they can to defend and support the regime. Because of the anger and resentment that other Cubans harbor toward these individuals, the choice for them truly may be socialism or death, as Fidel's down-fall could lead to violent retribution against them.

The Party faithful occupy the upper echelon of all professional endeavors. Members of this *nomenklatura* make their politics clear when talking with foreigners, sometimes bluntly stating, "I am a Marxist-Leninist." Despite this verbal loyalty to the regime, Cubans in official positions are animated and friendly in exchanging pleas-antries and discussing general topics. However, when a conversation touches upon politics and they begin to spout the Party line, the life in their eyes dies; there is no emotion behind the words. In trying to determine how loyal a Cuban is to the Revolution, the answer lies not in the words spoken but in the conviction with which they are said. It seems that over three decades of Revolution have resulted in not only a lack of consumer goods and freedom but also a scarcity of true loyalty to the regime.

The Party faithful are not the only ones who have a lot to lose if there is a change in the regime. The voluntarily unemployed, those who choose not to work, also do, for they would probably be de-prived of the benefits they currently receive. Candido, a thirty-four-year-old mulatto* with short dark hair and cinnamon-colored skin who works long hours to support his wife and two children said, "Do you know who supports the Revolution? The people who don't work. They know that if things change, they will have to work for a living. Now they do not have to do anything." There are a great many people on the island who do not work because they can get by without having a job; they live off the provisions of the State. Cubans who work do not think much of those who do not. Alberto, a light-skinned man in his late twenties who supports an extended family

---

* Mulatto is used here the way people in Cuba use it. It refers to a person of mixed European and African heritage. It does not have a negative connotation; it is merely descriptive.

by doing odd jobs, commented, "I live in a bad neighborhood. Next door there is an ongoing domino game. They don't work. They don't understand why I do. They just sit and drink and play dominoes from noon until two o'clock in the morning." Beyond these two groups, support for the regime runs thin.

On the other end of the political scale from the Party faithful are the dissidents, those rare individuals who live outside the system and actively oppose the State and Revolution. These individuals seek to improve the human rights situation on the island by calling attention to abuses and by educating fellow citizens. They suffer for their efforts. Most either have been fired or have left their jobs. (Almost all jobs in Cuba are sponsored by the State, so those who dissent inevitably have problems at work.) Many have spent time as political prisoners. They live hand to mouth, often off the charity of family and friends. These activists face a credible risk of being detained or imprisoned for their beliefs and political activities because Cuban law restricts freedom of association, information, and expression.

The largest group in Cuba consists of those who still have their jobs with the State and continue to function within the system but no longer believe in the Revolution. In the workplace they do what they must to survive, but in private they might express their real feelings. This *doble moral* (dual morality) is the key to how they cope with their political environment. In private, with those they trust, they express their true thoughts. In public, they are good revolutionaries. The economic necessity of employment demands that individuals go through the motions of political loyalty. Maintaining a *doble moral* allows individuals to mentally separate what they have to do to survive politically and economically from what they believe. Two journalists who personally expressed to me their sincere interest in the United States and their desire to travel there were experts at maintaining the *doble moral*. As trusted workers, they were allowed by their offices to attend functions sponsored by the U.S. Interests Section. On the airwaves, however, they stuck to the political hard line and condemned U.S. actions and society. It was what they had to do.

Political survival in Cuba is like a high-wire act. To survive, one needs to walk the line carefully, something a professor I knew at the University of Havana had learned to do admirably. I could tell how the winds were blowing at the university by noting whether or not Francisco would see me. On occasion he appeared unannounced at my doorstep. He would enjoy seven-year-old Havana Club rum, eat imported cheese, and ask to listen to music that reminded him of his youth. He would reminisce about his childhood and talk of topics with no political sensitivities. He was always cautious about what he said in my house, particularly if I asked about the university and the political mood. He knew we had an audience. In late summer 1996 I tried several times to see him at his home but to no avail. Although I left copies of academic journals and even a prized tin of Camembert cheese, he did not contact me. The climate at the university was tense at the time, so I am not surprised that he avoided me. It was too great a risk, and he had too much to lose. Another professor, the head of the Department of Philosophy at the university, Jorge Acanda, took one wrong step on the tightrope. He lost his position because he spoke his mind at an inopportune time. He made the mistake of speaking to a young *Chicago Tribune* reporter who was eager for a story. In an article published on April 7, 1996, Acanda was quoted as saying, "For many people today, Marxism means nothing." A comment like this from a person who is the head of a department and assumed to be extremely loyal to the Revolution makes good copy in the United States. In Cuba, such a remark hits like a bombshell and has serious consequences.

Academics are not alone in their walk on that thin line. Trusted Party officials can fall from grace for a misstep. In February 1995, the American Association of Publishers presented a ground-breaking exhibit of over six thousand American books at the old Capitol Building, which is now the Academy of Sciences. Though access to the building was restricted, the exhibit was well attended. Cubans sat poring over tomes on baseball and were fascinated by picture books and children's stories. The event was quite a success, opening a door between Cubans and Americans. Shortly after the exhibit closed, the director of the Cuban Book Institute, a staunch but effective Party man, was removed from his position. A source at the book institute claimed that the director was dismissed because Fidel had not given his approval for the exhibit in advance. However, any event of this magnitude could hardly have escaped the notice of the highest levels of the regime. Armando Hart, the minister of culture and a close advisor to Fidel, was present at the opening of the exhibit. Perhaps what Fidel did not like was the positive impact that the exhibit had inside Cuba and the press play that it received outside the country. Someone had to take the fall, and the director, despite his capability and loyalty, was that person.

Successfully navigating the political quagmire is crucial for Cubans because almost all of them work for the State, whether they are engineers, lawyers, professors, artists, or construction workers. Since the State is the source of employment and livelihood, Cubans find themselves obliged to follow the edicts that their places of employment give them about their behavior not only inside but also outside the office. One way this control is evident is in the need to receive permission from the workplace to attend receptions and dinners sponsored by diplomats. At one Fourth of July reception at the Principal Officer's residence, there were almost no Cubans in attendance, even though many had been invited. (The United States does not have an ambassador in Cuba; the Principal Officer fulfills that role.) Another reception at the same place held just two weeks later was very well attended. Some Cubans admitted that they had been barred from attending the U.S. Independence Day event.

Because the stakes are so high, Cubans are afraid of taking any action that might be misconstrued. The Castro regime effectively uses blackmail to create fear and keep people from acting against the regime. If there is something that the State can take from an individual—a professional opportunity, a child's position in a good school, permission to leave the country, a dollar earning job—it has power over that person. It is to this power that the Cubans succumb. The experience of Carmen, an artist whose home I visited many times, is an example of how the State can exercise that power. After I invited her to a party at my home, she was called in to the main office of the school where she taught and ordered not to attend the gathering. She was warned that all doors would close for her professionally if she went. Carmen had recently gone abroad to exhibit her paintings and had hopes of traveling again. Her career was taking off; her work had been displayed at several Cuban galleries, and her talent had been profiled in the press. An action as simple as going to a social function had become a point of deviance from the path of the Revolution and a threat to her future. She did not come to the party.

One of the most autonomous groups on the island, the Masons, has been active in Cuba for over one hundred years. However, like almost all individual Cubans, Masons must constantly weigh the risks of their actions. They have to conform to the demands of the State or face the consequences. Because of the Masons' historical ties to the United States, they began to develop a relationship with the U.S. Interests Section. At the same time, they were trying to reestablish some of their connections with overseas chapters of Masons. In the course of the relationship, the U.S. Information Service (USIS) office of the Interests Section donated books on baseball, history, environmental issues, and American government to the Masonic Library and invited the leadership of the organization to diplomatic receptions. The State was not pleased with the growing relationship between the Masons and the Interests Section. As a result, the Masons were closely scrutinized, they were warned not to attend functions, and, ultimately, three of the Masons' top leaders were called in for questioning. They were accused of working for the Central

Intelligence Agency (CIA). Shortly thereafter, State Security officials made a surprise visit to the Masonic Lodge and searched the library, where they found allegedly "counterrevolutionary" materials. The officials ordered the leadership of the Grand Masonic Lodge to remove the library director and try him in a Masonic tribunal. The State threatened to close down the library completely and possibly ban the entire fraternal organization if its demands were not met. The Masons wanted to continue operating and did not want to lose their library. The regime, of course, prevailed.

The fear of losing position or livelihood is usually enough to persuade people to comply with political demands. When that fear is not sufficient and individuals fail to observe the requirements of the regime, the State can detain them and potentially charge them with a political crime. Detention can last from a few hours to months on end. A detained Cuban may simply be instructed to sit in a chair for hours and wait, without even being given a glass of water. A person may also be detained and interrogated. Others are held for weeks or months in small cells without ever being formally charged with a crime. Three crimes that constitute a threat to the Cuban Revolution are *peligrosidad* (dangerousness), *desacato* (irreverence or defiance), and *propaganda enemiga* (enemy propaganda). *Peligrosidad* is so general that it applies in almost any circumstance. Disobeying a decree, speaking one's mind, or spending time with an American is as "dangerous" as throwing rocks at police officers. Contact with an American can be enough to warrant questioning. A Cuban friend, Carlos, was picked up by State Security and questioned as to whether he understood the high level of *peligrosidad* that he was running by spending time with me, an American. He displayed bravado by telling the authorities that he was not interested in my politics or theirs. He was shaken and very disturbed by the experience, uncertain of what the State could do to him. The authorities did not bother him again for almost two months, when they accused him of working for the CIA and threw him out of his job.

Desacato is often used against dissidents and independent thinkers. The charge implies disrespect to the Revolution and Fidel Castro. Graffiti, such as *Abajo Fidel* (Down with Fidel) or *Ab-Del* (an abbreviation of Down with Fidel), appears in tunnels, in elevators, and on walls but is quickly covered with the words *Viva Fidel*. One joke is that a teenager had written *Abajo F* on a wall when he was interrupted by the authorities. The young man claimed that he was trying to remember the American president's name—Flinton.

Propaganda enemiga can be charged against a Cuban for possession of a copy of the *Miami Herald,* the Universal Declaration of Human Rights, or any book about Cuba not blessed by the Castro regime. In American embassies and other diplomatic missions around the world, the USIS, the organization for which I worked, distributes materials on U.S. society, politics, and economics to the local population. In Havana, I was in charge of the distribution of materials and information about democracy and the functions of a free press, an independent judiciary, and free market economics. For the first year of my posting in Havana, USIS also distributed copies of the *Miami Herald* and *El Nuevo Herald.* Copies of these papers went to dissidents, independent journalists, the University of Havana, think tanks, the international edition of the Communist Party newspaper *Granma,* Radio Rebelde, and a few other choice institutions. When the Cuban government stopped clearing these papers through customs, we had to stop delivery. Interestingly enough, my office received calls from Party strongholds *Granma* and the University of Havana asking when they would start receiving the newspapers again. Possession of materials from the U.S. Interests Section is a convenient excuse for the State to detain those it wishes. On one occasion, an independent journalist, Roxana Valdivia, who is now living in the United States as a political refugee, was detained leaving my office with some books and several copies of *El Nuevo Herald* that she had requested. State Security threatened to charge her with *propaganda enemiga* and after some delay sent her back to her home in a provincial city.

Most Cubans are tired of politics because everything in their lives has been political. One afternoon, when I joined a group of forty-ish Cuban artists for lunch, all of us agreed not to discuss politics. When conversation on the subject of art and culture evolved toward the political and cultural relationship of the United States and Cuba, one man reminded us, "Hey, we said no politics!" The topic changed when someone asked me about horseback riding. I told them how much I was enjoying riding and how much I was learning. As I talked, I did not think about the fact that, in Cuba, "*El Caballo*" is one of the names given Fidel. In response, one man quipped, "So, you have learned to master the Horse (*El Caballo*) during your time in Cuba. If only we could do the same!"

Like the artists I was having lunch with, most Cubans in their thirties and forties have had their lives shaped by the Revolution. Participating in the literacy campaign as children, cutting cane, studying at the university, pursuing their professions, and then discovering their way blocked by political decisions, they either have ultimately reached a point of disenchantment with the system or have found a way to accept life with the *doble moral*. Luis, a professional in his forties who abandoned a career in the arts because of the demands of the powerful State, lamented, "We are the lost generation. Older people fought in the Revolution and pursued their dream. We have only experienced the Revolution. We did not hear rock and roll. We had dreams. When will we be able to pursue them? It is too late for us now. The younger ones will be able to pursue their dreams. But what about us?"

Because there is so much to lose by speaking out, most Cubans have adopted a position that allows them to go on with their professional lives while privately admitting their disappointment with the Revolution. At Estella's birthday party, a professor and an engineer, both in their forties, were chatting when the professor wiggled his index finger—a new hand symbol for me—as he said to me, "Here we are all like this." The engineer explained in one word, "*gu-sano*." In Spanish this word means worm, but in the Cuban vernacular it means counterrevolutionary. These two men were not dissidents. They were employed by the State, yet their hearts were not with the Revolution. Their actions, however, were not against it.

One evening Agustin, a thirty-five-year-old man with cinnamon skin and brown eyes, showed me photos of his family and friends. Among them was a black and white 8×10. When he saw it, he chuckled and said, "You won't believe this," and promptly covered half the picture. The photo was of a group of cane workers from the early years of the Revolution: "This is my father, and there I am— and guess who this is?" As he moved his hand, I saw that the man in the center of the photo was none other than Fidel Castro. Agustin's father had been part of a cane-cutting brigade that had won a productivity award. Fidel came personally to congratulate them. That small boy in a provincial cane field grew up to attend a university and went on to be a teacher. Even this man, who had benefited from the Revolution because he had secured an education and escaped a life of labor in the provinces, had no interest in politics.

The older people, too, who fought in the streets and supported the Revolution at the beginning, have silently stepped away from the regime. Few question or try to limit the activities of these "Heroes of the Revolution." Many of them pursue academic or other agendas that take them away from the political maelstrom. They have come to realize that all they strived for and fought for has become an illusive dream. For those who truly believed in the ideals of the Revolution, the reality of discovering that everything they had worked for has crumbled like the buildings of old Havana has been devastating. The other reality that haunts them is the bleak future for their children.

Cubans in their twenties and thirties have experienced nothing but the Revolution, and they are less than enamored of it. These young people see no future in Cuba because they see no way to make a living under the current system, and they cannot imagine political or economic change occurring. They do not really have a sense of what being Cuban means besides what the Soviets and Fidel have force-fed them. For them, Cuba, the *patria* (fatherland), has been linked to socialism, and socialism to Fidel. Disillusionment with any one of these elements leads to a lower regard for the others. The Union of Young Communists has tried to attract new adherents with dance parties and other activities but has met with little success. The leader of that group is well into her forties and hardly representative of the younger generation in which hip young men wear pony-tails and seek creative ways to leave the island.

Even though disenchantment with the Revolution is widespread, the State is still able to mobilize hundreds of thousands of people for May Day celebrations and anti-American marches down the Malecón. On the day of a parade, usually a holiday, all the employees of an enterprise show up to work or at another central location, where they might receive a new t-shirt, and then are transported by bus to the site of the march. Public transportation shuts down for the duration of the event because all resources are dedicated to transporting the masses to and from the demonstration. The streets are eerily quiet. Groups of people are funneled onto the main street of the march and they walk. Many leave as soon as they are allowed. A Cuban government march is a manifestation of the *doble moral* on a massive scale. Thousands act the part of good revolutionaries, all the time knowing that they would rather be spending their time securing necessities for their families. Instead, they serve the political necessity of feigned loyalty to an aging Revolution—and get a t-shirt.

< 2 >

No Es Fácil

Food and Daily Life

Have you heard the two reasons the pope wants to visit Cuba? He wants
to meet the devil in person and see a people living off miracles.
—joke from a devout Catholic

The phrase *"no es fácil"* (it isn't easy) is repeated like a mantra on the
island. That simple statement captures the challenge inherent in obtaining food and necessities while dealing with the trials of daily life.
Andrés, a dark-haired professional man in his mid-thirties who works
two jobs, captured the essence of this difficulty when he asked me
rhetorically, "Do you know the first thing most Cubans think about
when they wake up in the morning? What am I going to do for food
today?" His lament over the scarcity of food is symptomatic of the
economic troubles that began for Cuba with the collapse of the Soviet Union. Cuba is a heavily trade-dependent nation, and until the
dramatic changes occurred in Eastern Europe and the Soviet Union,
it had relied on its socialist brothers in those countries for most of
its trade. Between 1989 and 1992, Cuba lost about 70 percent of its
imports and exports. Facing this void, the island had to scramble to
find new trading partners. Doing so was not easy, because Cuba had
a huge hole in its economy, little hard currency, and not much to
sell.

In 1991, to respond to the new circumstances, Fidel Castro declared the beginning of the "Special Period in Time of Peace." In
wartime, citizens make sacrifices for their country. During the Special Period, people would have to go without many goods, as if they

were in a war. They would have less fuel, less food, less clothing, less everything. The draconian reality included acute food shortages, which led to outbreaks of malnutrition-related diseases, including one that causes blindness. The absence of medicine, including aspirin, meant turning to ancient herbal remedies for relief. The lack of gasoline meant that private automobiles virtually disappeared from the streets, and buses were rare and filled to capacity by people who had sometimes waited for hours at the bus stop. Bicycles became the most common form of transportation. People learned how to stay clean without soap and to care for their teeth without toothpaste. They became accustomed to standing in line for hours for a meager ration of rice and beans. The kind of deprivation they experienced would have destroyed many societies, but Cuban society held together. Although the situation has improved since the worst days of the early 1990s, there are still chronic shortages of goods and the State continues to have trouble providing basic services like garbage collection. It is also having trouble providing clothing, from school uniforms to women's underwear.

The scarcity of food is exemplified in the experience of Ana Maria, a playwright in Santiago de Cuba, who lives off a peso salary and depends, like most Cubans, on the food supplied by government rations. Gray-haired and rail-thin, she looked at me with sparkling, intelligent blue eyes as she chain smoked and related a story: "My mother lives with me. She does not go out any more because she is over eighty. She does not understand how things are. One day I had nothing to feed her for lunch except plain rice. When I gave it to her she asked, 'Couldn't you fry up an egg to go on top?' I said, 'Mama, I am sorry, but there are no eggs.' She ate the rice and said, 'Oh, that was so good. Could I please have some more?' 'Mama,' I said, 'I am so sorry, but there is no more.' Do you know how it felt not to be able to feed her a decent lunch? She does not understand how things are. We have nothing. Nothing."

Cubans receive a basic food ration from the State in accordance with the number and ages of people in the family. Most families subsist on this very limited bundle of goods. Children up to the age of seven receive a daily milk ration. Each person, regardless of his or her age, receives one piece of bread that resembles a hamburger bun every day. This bread is such a fixture in people's lives that a painting of one of these pieces of bread was displayed at an important national art show with the title "*Our Daily Bread.*" Such basic goods as cooking oil and soap have virtually disappeared from the ration card in the past few years. The meat that is distributed is the subject of jokes. And in this nation of coffee lovers, the ration of ground coffee beans for two weeks is a small three-by-four-inch bag. The coffee is purported to be mixed with ground-up peas, sawdust, or just about anything that will give it bulk. People have commented to me that they are not sure what real coffee looks or tastes like any more. The quality of goods distributed, however, is not as important a concern as the quantity of the items. The food allotment is not sufficient for feeding a family. An elementary school teacher commented to me, "There are parents sending their children to school with no breakfast because they have no food in the house." He went on to comment on his own situation: "Do you know what a single person receives on the ration card for the month? Almost nothing. If you really stretch, there is enough for ten days. You have no idea how difficult it is to live."

The average educated person earns a monthly salary of about 300 Cuban pesos, the equivalent of 15 U.S. dollars. Pensions run between 150 and 200 pesos. People pay for the goods in the ration, but the prices are quite low, so they are affordable. The coffee ration, for instance, costs twelve centavos of one peso. Special products like a jar of jam or a bottle of rum might be available for three or four pesos. The dry goods and meat are distributed from a neighborhood *bodega* (store). On the first of the month Cubans pick up rice, sugar, and beans. If a person does not go to the *bodega* on the first of the month, he or she may find nothing available the next day. Eggs and meat arrive on other days. Most people have to check at the *bodega* every day to see what has arrived. In families in which there is a retired or unemployed person who has time to stand in line and check on supplies, this is not so difficult, but for those who work and arrive home after the food distribution places close, finding the time can be complicated. Cubans have to go to three different places for the items on their ration card: the bakery for their daily bread, an agricultural market—not the same as the *agromercado* described later—for vegetables, and the *bodega* for dry goods and meat. It is not unusual that one area of a town will be two months behind on a sugar ration and another late on cigarettes. People trade and swap with those living in other districts to obtain the essentials they lack.

In the era of Soviet subsidies, Cubans did not have to worry about food. People raised during that time are tall, strong, and healthy. Today, however, birth weights are down. Parents of an American two-year-old were regularly asked if the child was four. Children learning to walk seem doll-sized, as few get the nutrition necessary to develop as they should. During a visit to a home on the eastern end of the island, I was handed a baby to hold. The baby's father was a handsome black man who danced professionally, and his mother was a slender blue-eyed white woman. I knew the baby had been ill, but his head was out of proportion to his body, and he resembled the extremely malnourished children seen in areas of famine. The child seemed to be the size of a four-month-old, but he was performing skills no four-month-old baby could. I learned that, indeed, the child was nine months old. The baby had needed a special formula, which the doctor had prescribed. However, the formula was unavailable, so the people distributing rations gave the family dry milk instead. The milk caused a severe reaction in the child, who became critically ill, was hospitalized for an extended period, and barely clung to life.

The declaration of the Special Period required the State to make some changes that would allow the country to muddle through. These measures were deviations from the socialist path and will have long-term effects on Cuban socialism. One major change occurred in 1993, when the State made it legal for ordinary citizens to hold dollars, an action that previously had resulted in imprisonment. People with family overseas could now use dollars sent to them by their relatives, and people fortunate enough to work for embassies or foreign businesses could earn dollar bonuses. To give Cubans a place to spend these newly acquired funds, the State allowed them access to certain special stores where goods were available only for dollars. These stores had previously been reserved for diplomats and other foreigners residing in Cuba. Permitting individual Cubans to hold dollars quickly led to the creation of a dollar or high-cost-peso economy that exists parallel to the established nonconvertible peso economy.

In addition, the regime allowed the first signs of private enterprise, permitting people to become "self-employed" in certain areas of the economy. By 1996 government figures put the number of self-employed workers at about 200,000, and many of those who were self-employed were working for dollars. All of these economic steps gave birth to a fissure in Cuban society between the haves and the have-nots. This gap may yet haunt the regime, as the socialist goal of equality continues to be undermined by the State's policies.

In 1994, to ease the food shortage and stimulate private production, Raul Castro pushed for the return of free, as opposed to State-run, agricultural markets where private vendors could sell produce for a profit. The idea had been tried briefly in 1986 and then abandoned. As the head of the armed forces, Raul Castro was pragmatic enough to realize that the country's most important national security issue was feeding the people. With the opening of the *agromercados,* the people had a food source other than the State ration card and the dollar store. Prices at the markets are high, but the *agromercados* offer shoppers fruit, vegetables, pork, beans, and some prepared items. Although few people can afford to buy much when a pound of pork is 25 pesos and a good month's salary is only 300 pesos, peso-earning Cubans can purchase some food, even if only one pepper or tomato, to put on the table.

The *agromercados* were intended to stimulate private production, but supply to the markets comes, to a large degree, from the huge state farms. Relatively little comes from private farmers. To sell at the *agros,* a vendor has to pay the government an exorbitant fee to rent a stall, which means he cannot pay top dollar for the farmer's goods and hope to break even. For small farmers such as José, an exuberant man who proudly shows visitors through his lush garden of paradise that boasts mango and avocado trees, green beans, papaya, tomatoes, peppers, and a small grape vineyard, the more lucrative option is to sell produce to the vendors who go door-to-door with the wares. Although door-to-door vendors are supposed to be licensed by the State, they tend to duck this regulation and thereby avoid paying the State its percentage. Since they do not give the State its cut, they can afford to pay the small farmer more money for his quality goods.

Even though Cubans cannot afford to buy more than a few items at *agromercados,* the markets are busy centers of activity. Most neighborhoods in Havana have an *agromercado,* as do the towns and cities in the provinces. In Havana Vieja, I knew I was nearing an *agro* because of the increase in foot traffic and noise. The building that housed the *agro* had been used as a market for generations, and the antique scales for weighing the goods were American made and imported well before the Revolution. Prices were written in chalk on black slates and posted above the wooden bins. The sharp smell of butchered meat hung in the air as I wandered through the crowded market, stepping carefully over decomposing bits of fruits and vegetables. Vendors hawked their pineapples, peppers, and yucca, urging me to buy. On the other end of the island, in the town of Guantanamo, not far from the no-man's-land that separates Cubans from the United States military base of Guantanamo, the *agro* was not as well supplied or as busy as those in Havana. In this place where tourist dollars were scarce and few people earned dollars for their work, there was not much for sale at the open-air market the day I went there besides a tuber called *boniato,* onions, and bananas. The entire supply of pork had been sold earlier in the day. A truck loaded with corn from a State farm had just rumbled in and was being unloaded. Outside the market, a middle-aged private farmer with deep wrinkles around his eyes held green peppers in his hands for sale. A twenty-year-old black man sat at a makeshift table refilling disposable lighters with a variant of bug spray.

Perhaps the most prosperous market I saw on the island was in Matanzas. Lying about an hour east of Havana, the city was reaping the hard currency benefits of being near the tourist beach mecca of Varadero. Many of its young residents had found jobs at the tourist hotels and were filling the pockets of their families with dollars. The large market square, crowded with shoppers and filled with produce, gave the impression that one was no longer in a socialist country. As I shopped there, contemporary American rap music blared over the loudspeaker, which had probably been installed years before to broadcast political speeches. There was an air of relative prosperity; people ate ice cream and socialized as they went about their business. The entire square was dedicated to the market. To one side, there were wooden stalls where people sold cooked meals and hot coffee in the ninety degree heat. Nearby, vendors were selling fresh red snapper and other fish. Trucks with canopies were lined up in a row, the truck beds serving as platforms from which young men sold melons, plantains, and okra. Old men sat smoking cigarettes on empty wooden crates as they watched shoppers fill their bags. In the midst of the bustle, a light-skinned woman with straight brown hair approached me quietly and asked if I would buy the gold necklace she was wearing. On the far side of the market were three horse-drawn wagons. A deeply tanned, ageless man with three days' growth of gray beard, who sported a straw cowboy hat and chomped on the stump of a cigar, stood beside the wagons. Willing to give a ride for one peso, he was the taxi service.

Back in Havana, people fortunate enough to have access to dollars were spending their money at dollar stores, the best known of which is the *diplotienda* (diplomats' store). This grocery store, located near the Russian (formerly Soviet) Embassy, was once reserved solely for diplomats and other foreigners. Cubans were admitted only after it became legal to hold dollars. Run by the State, the store sells milk, eggs, meat, ice cream, bread, fruit, vegetables, imported cheese and butter, and canned and dry goods. There is a catch: The store accepts only dollars, and lots of dollars are required because the prices are very high. For the foreigner, the *diplotienda* is a poorly stocked, crowded, smelly, unpleasant place. For the locals, shopping there is a privilege and a rare event. Cubans with dollars go there for essentials like cooking oil and meat that they cannot get elsewhere. Inside the *diplotienda,* one of the most crowded places is the cold bin where the hamburger is placed. One Saturday, the bin was completely empty when Julio, a thin fifty-year-old black man with a ready smile who worked in the meat section, pushed a cart toward it. A group, which included me, descended like vultures on the cart, fighting for the packets of hamburger, worried there would be none left.

To put the challenges a Cuban faces for food in perspective, one need only consider the behavior of foreigners who have enough money to buy supplies at the dollar stores. Hoarding, for instance, is common. People will buy and store items like butter, cocoa, and sugar because they do not know when supplies will dwindle. At the *diplotienda,* one of the only reliable sources of flour in Havana, weeks often passed without flour on the shelves. On my first visit to the store, I was sagely advised by the person I was shopping with to purchase multiple loaves of bread and a ten-pound brick of Swiss cheese because it was rare to find bread and rarer still to find cheese. I eventually made my own bread because the supply at the store was irregular and of poor quality. At times, certain goods like butter and toilet paper could not be found, for any price, anywhere in the city.

Although most foreigners could buy food with dollars and often stocked their pantries with hard-to-find staple goods, finding all the ingredients for meals was a challenge. An American friend, Karin, who was on her first Foreign Service assignment, wanted to fix a bacon, lettuce, and tomato sandwich and then realized she did not have the ingredients and could not get some of them. In Cuba, the fruits and vegetables for sale are those that happen to be in season. Tomatoes, lettuce, carrots, avocados, mangoes, and potatoes have their seasons, even in the tropics. Bananas, pineapples, and green beans are available year round, but even when a fruit or vegetable is in season and for sale, neither its quantity nor its quality is dependable. I was impressed when someone could get together the ingredients for a real salad; tomatoes, lettuce, carrots, and cucumber in the same bowl was a big event.

Cubans obtain most of their food through the legal sources of the ration card, the *agromercados,* and the dollar grocery stores. It is, however, impossible to ignore the contribution of the thriving illegal black market. Men and women knock on doors around neighborhoods offering everything from lobster (at a dollar a tail) to bananas. Goods are stolen from State warehouses and dollar stores and sold. Multi-gallon containers of ice cream waltz out the back door of the Coppelia Ice Cream Shop (the famous opening and closing location in the Academy Award nominated movie *Fresa y Chocolate*) and into the freezers of private restaurants and individuals. Bacon and ham from dollar stores and relief shipments show up for sale for dollars. Eggs are sold on the street at a slight discount from retail prices. Coffee, stolen from warehouses and packaging plants, is marketed at a fraction of its non-black-market asking price. Gasoline mixed with kerosene is sold at a discounted price. This buying and selling in the unofficial market keeps the system going and puts food on many tables. The theft of items from State warehouses can have disturbing consequences, however. In August 1996, several people were poisoned by eating a pizza sold on the street. The self-employed pizza maker had purchased stolen "flour" that was, in actuality, a poisonous potassium compound.

The black market will continue to survive as long as basic goods are beyond the resources of many and as long as items can be bought on the street for half the price charged in stores. Trading on the black market and stealing goods to sell are economic crimes because they threaten the socialist economy. However, without the black market goods, most Cubans would be much worse off. So warehouses and stockrooms are pilfered, the items are sold, and Cuban consumers get what they need while the middlemen earn some profit. The only loser is the State. But then again, if this black marketing is keeping people fed, is it not also contributing to the economy and helping maintain political stability for the State?

< 3 >

Hay Que Resolver

Working for Pesos and Dollars

Faced with the inescapable hardships and scarcities of daily life, Cubans have become supremely talented at making do and have displayed tremendous creativity in obtaining what goods they can. To *resolver* is to find a solution to a problem. On the island, "*resolver*" is more than a word; it is an art form. It may involve finding the necessities for a newborn baby, obtaining a cup of oil, or getting the telephone fixed. It is dealing with the shortages and getting by in the face of unrelenting economic difficulties. People *resolver* through access to a few dollars, the help of friends and family, creative minds, hard work, and luck.

Cubans can be separated into three economic groups: those living off pesos; those also receiving some dollar income, either through jobs in the dollar sector or family remittances; and the "newly rich," who are either self-employed or have ties to the *nomenklatura* and have enough dollars to consume conspicuously. Anyone working for the State, including doctors, lawyers, professors, economists, journalists, artists, musicians, architects, sugarcane cutters, factory workers, and carpenters, earns a peso salary. They have to *resolver* more than the other groups to make ends meet. Completely dependent on the State for their livelihood, they live off the goods supplied by the ration card. It is hard for Westerners to understand their daily struggle for survival, because most of us have never known hunger. Our lives are filled with electronic gadgets, while Cubans scrounge for candles to burn during the unscheduled and often lengthy electrical blackouts.

For some, often the most needy, life is characterized by compromise and inevitably doing without. Gloria, a soft-spoken mulatta in her mid-thirties who earns only pesos, is a case in point. A single mother of two children, she lives in a neighborhood known for crime. Her tiny home lies at the end of a long, dark corridor that is open to the elements. Drops of water from a recent storm fell on my head as I walked down the narrow way, past the open doors of apartments where residents were watching television. Gloria and her family live in a windowless one-room space with a ladder heading up to a loft. When school started and new uniforms were not available, Gloria had to send her eight-year-old son to class in his old maroon school uniform, which was too small and worn completely through the seat. There was no way for her to patch the holes. The boy's tennis shoes had holes in the toes so large that no shoe remained below the laces. Her attractive fourteen-year-old daughter was wearing mismatched clothes that were a size too small. The family has a dog, but they have almost nothing to feed it; most days, they do not have enough food for themselves.

The State is having trouble providing even for its wounded war veterans. In the Plaza de la Catedral in Havana Vieja one Saturday, I met Manuel, a black man in his thirties. When we saw each other, we knew we had something in common, because he is missing one hand and most of his forearm and so am I. After I explained that I had been born with one hand, he told me his story. "I was a soldier in Angola. The bus I was on hit a mine. All of the other soldiers were killed or badly burned. I was very lucky. God was watching over me. I only lost my arm." In support of international revolution, Cuba has sent troops to countries in Latin America and Africa, including many troops sent to Angola. I asked Manuel if he had a job and whether the State was taking care of him. He was not working. He said, "I live here in Havana Vieja and have two daughters. It is very difficult. The money I receive as a veteran is barely enough to buy clothes. *No es fácil.*"

For those living off pesos, it is not easy to offer a visitor a precious cup of coffee, and yet when my hosts had some coffee in the house, they never failed to offer it to me. I did not like to ask for refreshment at Cuban homes because I knew how little my hosts had and how willingly they would give that little bit away. Even drinking water was a challenge for them at times, because the water supply in Havana sometimes carries health-threatening impurities. Some people boil their water to remove bacteria and other impurities; others take their chances. When I asked for a glass of water at one friend's house, he said, "I do not think you want water because mine comes straight from the tap. Please let me make coffee." It was near the beginning of the month, so he still had coffee left from the ration. On other visits, he had nothing to offer but conversation. On the other end of the island, Gladys, a retired pharmacist whose brother once attended the Massachusetts Institute of Technology, lived surrounded by a wealth of museum quality antiques, but she had no money for fruit or vegetables; she was limited to the ration card. Yet in a show of Cuban generosity, she shared with visitors the first pieces of fruit she had in weeks. She made the best she could of her world. She had a well-used antique kerosene lamp ready to light when the power went off at night. Because she had difficulty going down stairs, she had rigged up a pulley system that allowed her to open the front door at the bottom of the stairs from where she stood at the top.

The inventiveness of Gladys's pulley system is mirrored in the creative approach many people take to using the items they have to create or build what they need. Isabel, a sculptor, lives with her mother and son. Many years ago, the warehouse-style building in which they live had been her father's art studio. Now it is both studio and home. Isabel sculpts using materials few artists would think of employing to create beauty. She carves delicate and detailed figures of women out of beeswax, a material she can obtain on her peso salary. She also scrounges for old bottles and interesting shards of broken glass, incorporating them into her work. In one of her works, a whimsical devil sits on top of an antique druggist's jar that imprisons a beautiful fairy, complete with wings.

Working for pesos is discouraging, because the few pesos one receives for long hours of work purchase almost nothing. Jorge, a twenty-year-old auto mechanic who lives with his father in Santiago de Cuba, told me, "I make 148 pesos a month [$7.50 U.S.] at a full-time job. I like to work, I want to work. But I also want to see the fruits of my labor. See this pack of cigarettes? It cost me 10 pesos. How can I even think about marrying and raising a family when I cannot even support myself?" Jorge's experience is shared by many. Most young people wonder how they can ever *resolver* their economic futures while restricted to peso incomes. Alicia, a tall woman in her fifties with large brown eyes and black hair, has three grown children who have professional jobs. All three live with her and depend on her dollar salary. She told me, "The one who is a doctor makes 340 pesos [$17 U.S.] a month, a very good salary, but she cannot live on that. I am supporting them. They are all so frustrated. What did they study for? They cannot make a living."

Of all people earning pesos, sugarcane workers may carry the worst burden, for they do backbreaking labor that is intimately tied to the economic health of the nation. Driving through cane fields, a visitor gets a sense of the amount of labor needed to harvest cane by hand. Large muscular men, their backs shiny with sweat, swing relentlessly at the cane with machetes. Sugar is, and has historically been, Cuba's most important crop. Through the years, it has been exported in great quantity to the island's most important trading partners: first to Spain, later to the United States, then to the Soviet Union. When there was doubt about the sugar harvest meeting the optimistic target yield in 1996, Fidel roundly criticized the cane workers for not producing enough. His comments did not make them happy, particularly because of their dreadful working conditions. Some were laboring barefoot, and many had no access to decent meals. Word of their discontent was widespread and might have reached Fidel, for he later praised the workers, perhaps attempting to make up for his previous comments. As one older woman noted, "If there is no sugar, there is no country."

During a trip to check on the status of Cuban rafters who were returned to the island following the migration accords in 1995, I visited the home of cane workers on a sugar plantation near Banes, in eastern Cuba. Seeing their living situation, I could understand why one of the people who lived there had decided to try to raft to the United States. Two rickety wooden structures housed the extended family. The walls of the houses were boards slapped together, leaving large gaps that would not keep out wind or rain. The social area was outside and consisted of an assortment of stools and chairs, several without seats, around a makeshift table. One of the women of the family was scrubbing clothes on a broken slab of concrete in a tub in the yard. She and her sister cooked for the entire family outside over an open fire. The women shared the home with their husbands, father, brothers, and small children. I knew that earlier in the year the State had offered an incentive to workers—special coupons with which they could buy items usually available only for dollars. When I asked the younger sister what she thought about the initiative, she said, "It's good that we have these coupons now. I was able to get shoes for my children."

To *resolver* the difficulties of life as a peso-earning State employee, one has several options, and all revolve around dollars. The most common is to have family living abroad who send money. This money may be one of the key reasons many Cuban families have survived. From the Miami area alone, millions of dollars in remittances flow to Cuba each year. From the overseas relatives come, as well, precious gifts of medicine and clothing. On October 6, 1995, President Bill Clinton relaxed travel restrictions for Cuban expatriates, allowing them to return to Cuba once a year for humanitarian purposes without applying for special permission. Before this change, only two to three flights left Miami for Cuba each week. An odd assortment of people and objects traveled on those charters, and all travelers had to go through a lengthy process to obtain a license from the Treasury Department for travel to Cuba. Journalists, U.S. government employees on official assignment, diplomats, and academics sat side-by-side with elderly Cuban Americans on the limited flights to Cuba. The people of Cuban heritage carried lanterns, dolls, and silk flowers. Some women wore several hair bows, and most men wore at least one hat. All carried overstuffed duffel bags that had been dutifully enclosed in plastic wrap to repel rain and discourage thieves.

With the relaxation of the travel restriction, demand for charter flights grew some 300 percent and flights from Miami began arriving daily in Havana. Cubans living in the United States, who now had only to fill out a form at the airport to be licensed for travel, began to pour onto the island. Everyone in Cuba, it seemed, knew someone who was visiting from the United States. Rollerblades appeared on the streets. Many people were suddenly better dressed. Medicines, clothes, and money were flowing in and alleviating the material needs of those people fortunate enough to have family in America. The people arriving on the flights to the island were not only growing in number but also were changing demographically. The majority were still elderly, but there were also children, middle-aged folks, and young people. There were the rich and the not so rich. While some men still wore multiple hats—one I saw wore a baseball cap on top of a cowboy hat—it was the marked increase in the number of bags they carried that caught my attention. One couple had seventeen bags, but the average number seemed to be about five per couple. Many of the travelers looked as if they might have been bound for any number of Latin American or Caribbean countries, but their huge amount of luggage set them apart. In addition to carrying goods, they often carried large amounts of money to be distributed among relatives. On the planes, there was a palpable sense of expectation and joy at the prospect of seeing family members and sharing the treasures. Passengers applauded as the planes touched ground.

Working for Dollars

If a peso-earning Cuban cannot depend on relatives in America for funds, he or she might pursue employment options that provide dollar income. Two possibilities are obtaining one of the highly coveted jobs in the tourism and dollar sector and joining the ranks of the self-employed. Still, earning dollars is not a panacea. In the summer of 1996, a professional woman lamented, "Things are getting so bad. I am earning dollars, but I'm supporting my daughters, my mother, and someone who has lived with our family for years. I can barely make ends meet. I do not know how those with only pesos are living." Behind the crumbling facades of elegant buildings live Cubans who eke out a desperate existence. In most households, several generations live together in small apartments. Grown children cannot move out; there is no place for them to go, since there is a housing shortage. More than one marriage has broken up because the spouse and in-laws, living under the same roof, could not get along. Miles of gracious mansions line Fifth Avenue in Havana, but these are home to embassies, foreign businesses, and Cuban think-tanks. Most of the large houses were subdivided into small apartments long ago or are used for schools or offices.

The once elegant apartment houses are not kept up. While individual apartments may be in good shape, the common areas are in serious disrepair. After visiting with a friend in her airy, clean apartment, which was equipped with a stereo, television, and videocassette recorder, I waited with her for the elevator in the dark hallway. She told me she had replaced the lightbulbs in the hallway, but someone had stolen them within just a few days. She said, "I tried to do something to make this place more livable, but look what happened. No one wants anything in the public area to be cared for. They just want everyone to be miserable." The elevator did not come, so she turned on her flashlight and with lament showed me to the stairs. I discovered quickly why she had not wanted to take the stairs. The stairway was illuminated only by my friend's flashlight, but the darkness did not obscure the filth. Dog droppings dotted the landings, and the air was heavy with the stench of excrement.

Most smaller homes are also in need of repair. The problem is that few building materials are available except on the black market, and the State has cracked down on the illegal sales. David, who receives money from relatives in the United States, explained, "I need to repair the house, and I have the money to do it. The only problem is, everything comes off the black market. These days, if you fix up your house, State Security comes and asks you where you got the money and then asks you to show receipts for anything you bought. It is no wonder no one is fixing up their houses and everything looks like this." So, while he could *resolver* the repairs, David knew the government would be suspicious: "They do not want anyone to start improving his lot in life."

A Cuban who earns dollars inevitably supports an extended family. One woman explained this phenomenon by saying that people like her, who earn dollars, wear Superman's cape. "Superman," she said, "once came to Cuba. When he was ready to take off, he tried to leave the ground and couldn't. He tried again and was puzzled because something was sapping his strength. He even wondered whether Cuba had Kryptonite. Finally, he turned around to see why he could not fly. He was grounded because ten thousand Cubans were clinging to his cape!" She summed up her story by saying, "All of us have people who depend on us."

The jobs in the dollar sector are found in joint-venture firms, embassies, and the tourism industry. Since the State is trying to attract foreign investment, it has allowed foreign firms to establish joint-venture operations. These are ventures in which the foreign partner provides some capital and management expertise and the Cuban partner supplies labor, land, and the facility. At this point, the Spanish are investing in tourism with several Meliá hotels on the island, the Mexicans have invested in telephones and cement, and the Canadians have invested in mining. Joint-venture firms and embassies are lucrative places to work because of the bonuses that the firms pay directly to local employees in addition to the State peso salary. The bonuses can be soap and shampoo, but they might also be as much as 200 U.S. dollars per month. Jobs in tourism have two additional benefits: tips in dollars and access to foreigners. The access to foreigners is seen as a way off the island, because some tourists marry Cubans.

The foreign firms and diplomatic missions operating on the island cannot freely hire their employees. Instead, the State has an employment agency that provides lists of job candidates to these institutions. The business or mission selects the employee from the lists presented by the State. The business pays the salary of these workers in dollars, often hundreds of dollars, to the Cuban government. The workers are then paid in pesos, not dollars, and invariably they receive only a tiny fraction of the hard currency salary paid. The State takes most of the money. If the State feels a worker is no longer suitable, the worker's contract is terminated. Though the foreign business pays for the employees' services, the State actually pays the salaries and permits the workers to continue in their coveted employment. As a result, the employees' loyalty is first to the State and then to the firm.

A good command of English is one key to these jobs in the dollar sector; another is either a well-connected parent or a spotless record as a Revolutionary. Because English is seen as a way to potentially access dollars, there has been a surge in the number of people who want to learn to speak it. At the same time, the number of English teachers is dropping, since many of the best English speakers on the island, who had been teachers, have left their positions in academia to seek their fortunes in tourism. The promise of earning dollars draws people out of their chosen fields into the service sector. A waiter in the newly restored Casa Granda Hotel in Santiago de Cuba is actually trained as a mechanical engineer. A bartender is an English teacher. The taxi driver is a doctor.

Cuenta Propia

If a job in tourism or a joint venture is not feasible, another possibility is working *"cuenta propia,"* or self-employment. The government allows people to work legally on their own in certain areas. Self-employment serves the State's needs in two ways: It lets individuals fill in the gaps in services the State cannot provide—or does not need to provide—and it gives individuals who have been dismissed from their State jobs because of cutbacks a way to find a livelihood. Cubans can park bicycles, run a small restaurant, clip poodles, sell drinks or food on the street, or make and sell handicrafts. Laws, however, ban professionals from working privately in their area of training. A doctor, potentially, could groom dogs or park bicycles but could not legally make house calls or open a private medical office. If professionals wish to work in their area of expertise, they must work for the State at a peso salary. Nevertheless, despite the potential risk, some doctors, dentists, and veterinarians are moonlighting in their professions. To make ends meet, these highly educated professionals have resorted to making illegal house calls to foreigners and others who pay in dollars.

According to Cuban government figures, about 200,000 people are self-employed. Each is licensed by the State, must pay taxes, and must carefully avoid "illicit enrichment"—that is, they must not make too much money. While the State has given the green light to this limited private enterprise, the law against illicit enrichment stands because the Revolution is not keen on seeing a business class emerge. Still, the promise of a good income lures people into independent endeavors. A man I met who was selling vegetables had studied computer technology in Czechoslovakia. The owner of a private restaurant was a neurosurgeon. Another was a university professor. These self-employed workers may become a headache for the regime, because as they become more successful, they become less dependent on the State for their livelihood and less tied to the requirements of loyalty to the regime.

For some, being self-employed is not lucrative, just a means to survive economically. A pregnant black woman came to my door with her five-year-old daughter one evening about nine trying to sell potatoes. She told me wearily that she had been trying to sell the potatoes all day at the going rate, four dollars, with no success. She offered them to me for three dollars and said, "Please, I need to buy a cradle. I don't have a cradle, and I need this money to buy it." After I paid for the potatoes, she asked, "Could you please give my daughter a piece of bread? She has been with me all day. She has not eaten." I put together some food for them. The woman's response was not a big smile. It was a look of relief and a change of demeanor. She straightened her shoulders, which had been sagging, and when she looked at me there was a light in her eyes that had not been there before.

Self-employment covers a wide range of endeavors. Selling homemade wares is the most basic form. One Saturday, a wizened campesino, with sun-baked skin and a straw hat, appeared at my front door selling rakes he had made by hand. He said he had come a long way, from Guanabacoa, far on the other side of Havana. He explained, "A man in your neighborhood asked me to make these, but now he doesn't want to buy them." The old man continued, "They are well made. Look, there is even a hole so you can attach the wooden handle. They are only a dollar. Would you buy one?" I bought one. Before he left, he asked if I had any extra shoes. His shoes, he said, were no good, and he could not buy new ones because they were sold only for dollars and were very expensive. He went on his way, hawking his rakes as he shuffled away from my door.

The other end of the spectrum of self-employment is occupied by private restaurants, called *paladares*. These enterprises are family businesses. Though they can legally have no more than twelve seats and all the employees must be related to the owner, *paladares* have sprung up all over the country. All employees must be relatives because only the State employs people; one Cuban cannot employ another. The twelve-seat restriction is in place so the restaurants do not grow too large. However, owners of *paladares* are creative in getting around the rules the State has laid down. It is amazing, for instance, how many cousins and uncles a person can have who show no family resemblance. Some *paladares* have a front room with twelve seats and a back room with any number of additional tables. Though they are banned from selling shellfish because all lobster and shrimp are the property of the State, many of the restaurants simply do not list these items on the menu—the waiter, if asked, will provide the details.

The name *paladar* comes from the name of a heroine of a Brazilian soap opera that was popular in Cuba when these restaurants first opened. Some *paladares* are no more than one room in a house. Others are romantic garden settings or tropical settings under thatched palm roofs. The small ones have a homey feel, because diners are often eating in someone's living room, while the fancy ones rival restaurants in any Latin American city. Though these restaurants are not permitted to advertise, business cards are handed out and people spread the news about good ones. The owners of *paladares* have a specific kind of clientele they are trying to attract. Some aim at business from the tourist sector. Others appeal to Cubans with dollar salaries, and still others target average people and charge in pesos. At a *paladar* for tourists, a dinner that included an appetizer of fish cocktail, a fillet of red snapper, dessert, and a bottle of wine for two when I was in Cuba would cost about twenty U.S. dollars. These establishments did quite well, because the service and the food were better than that at the tourist hotels. At a more moderate *paladar,* pork, rice, beans, salad, and a beer would cost about seven U.S. dollars for two. For a Cuban family with access to dollars, a special occasion might merit a visit to one of the moderate *paladares*. The *paladares* that charged pesos were the least expensive and offered simple meals. For those who sold food for pesos on the street, pizza was popular because the ingredients were inexpensive.

Because the prices at many *paladares* are affordable, these restaurants fill an important niche. They give people a place to go, and they spawn jobs. Many a man, young and old, black and white, offered to watch my car while I dined. *Paladares* were opening all over the island until the State announced high taxes. Many of the less successful places closed their doors because they knew they could not make it financially. A successful *paladar* with a tourist clientele, however, could gross over five hundred dollars in one night—a fortune in Cuba. It is no wonder the State had to slap on taxes.

Selling whatever is available has become an art form. The mango tree in my backyard had many uses. It gave shade, gave my kitten access to the roof, and provided a living for some of my neighbors for a week or two. Though the tree was laden with mangoes—it was a good year—I did not eat many mangoes from my tree. My neighbors earned more than a week's wage by selling what they harvested in my yard. One Sunday morning, I heard noise coming from my roof. I went out my back door to discover one man on my roof, another in a tree, and a third looking over the eight-foot-high wall that surrounded my back yard. I shooed them away, asking who gave them permission to pick mangoes in my yard. A little later I heard them again and headed to my back door, only to hear, "She's coming!" and see them disappearing over the wall. They returned when I was not home and cleaned the tree. They also cleaned the tree on the other side of the fence. I saw one man in the tree and heard him encouraging the others to join him in picking the mangoes. "Come on," he said, "you need to earn a living."

La Jinetera

Many young women, out of economic necessity, have taken a more desperate route to making dollars. Working as prostitutes, called *jineteras* in the Cuban vernacular, attractive young women in provocative clothing ply their trade on street corners, near hotels, and in nightclubs. During the day, broad Quinta Avenida, or Fifth Avenue, is Havana's main thoroughfare for vehicles and a favorite place for people to stroll or exercise. At night, however, the boulevard, lined with palm trees and miles of elegant mansions, is one of the preferred venues of the *jineteras.*

Old-timers will freely admit that there were prostitutes before the Revolution, but they insist that there were not this many and they were not so visible. Prostitution was one of the vices that the Revolution fought in its early years, and it was successful in eliminating the trade. One woman who as a student fought in the streets for Fidel worked with prostitutes in the early 1960s, educating and training them for jobs, and helping them enter society. Now she sees her work as being for naught because, though the Revolution claimed to have eradicated prostitution, the State has allowed it to flourish again. To promote tourism, the government has been selling Cuba as a sexual paradise, using photos of scantily clad beautiful women to entice tourists. During a talk show on State-controlled Radio Rebelde one evening, the commentators were discussing how tourists were favorably impressed with the island when one remarked: "They said our people are very courteous and even our prostitutes are educated." In 1995, the Italian magazine *Viaggiare* rated Cuba the number one country in the world for sex tourism.

Some like to say that the young women are getting involved in prostitution because they like to lead a wild life. The more realistic know that it is a way to survive. On the veranda of a tourist hotel I stayed in on the eastern end of the island, almost all of the tables were occupied by European and Asian men with *jineteras*. A few European women were sharing drinks with very attractive dark-skinned Cuban men at the other tables. Referring to the *jineteras,* Roberto, a musician in his fifties who plays guitar at the hotel, shook his head and commented, "I hate seeing them with these old fat men. Their parents know what they are doing, but what can they say when their daughter is bringing home soap and cooking oil and shampoo?" When I asked a twenty-year-old blonde *jinetera* about her situation, she said bluntly, "You adapt." Another, a lovely mulatta, said, "Who is going to feed our mothers? A lot of us have children. Who is going to feed them? I have a three-year-old girl at home." These are attractive, educated Cuban women and girls, in all the colors of the rainbow, who are servicing the needs of paunchy, licentious tourists from around the world. Some of the tourists marry the girls and take them away; others buy a few gifts and leave some dollars. The women are working as prostitutes because they need the money to feed their families.

In Havana, the Copacabana is still a hot spot where "music and passion" are the fashion, but I did not see anyone there with "feathers in her hair." I did, however, see some interesting outfits. The club at the Copacabana Hotel started hopping close to midnight. One night when I was there, the *jineteras* were out in force wearing spandex mini dresses with clunky platform shoes. They moved their bodies in ways that defy description—little jerks of their hips that made their bodies look as if they were vibrating. As they thrust themselves against their foreign dancing partners, they made their sexual interests clear. One shimmied her backside against her partner's groin; another worked herself up her man's leg. One European dropped to his knees, placing his face in the waist-deep cleavage of his partner's dress. The *jinetera* in a white vinyl skirt got her man, as did the one wearing lace bike shorts. The woman with bleached blond hair wearing red spandex over a plump body was the least appealing of the group, but even she got her man. The women were dressing for all tastes, some in blue jeans, others in frilly cotton dresses, most in sexy, short, form-fitting garments, but they all found what they were pursuing.

The Hotel Riviera with its Palacio de la Salsa and its 1950s decor is a mecca for tourists and *jineteras*. The line of people waiting to get into, or to be escorted into, the club is always long. The Palacio is famous because the best salsa bands on the island perform there every weekend. One Saturday night when I went dancing at the Palacio with a group of friends, I watched the enormous ballroom fill to capacity. On the dance floor, middle-aged Europeans moved stiffly beside statuesque mulattas. In the aisles, sexily dressed young women moved to the music, trying to attract the interest of a john. Groups of male tourists sat together, gradually acquiring women as the night progressed. At one point during the evening's show, a few women were invited on stage to dance. When one lifted her skirt and showed her assets to the crowd, I was not surprised. As we left, I commented to my American companion that I thought at least 75 percent of the women in the place either were bought and paid for or would be by the end of the evening. His retort was, "More like 90 percent."

It is not just the women who provide services. One evening when I was in the resort area of Varadero, I went to a discotheque with friends. The place was packed with male tourists and *jineteras*. When my friends left me to go dance, a most attractive twenty-twoish blue-eyed man with cinnamon-colored skin approached me and tried to offer his companionship. "*Ay, Bella*" he crooned as he stroked my arm. I declined the invitation, but I am sure he found another foreign woman to accompany. The *jineteras* will also offer their services to women. I saw a young woman outside a hotel say good-bye to a john and then turn around and proposition a female American professor.

Unfortunately, the girls in the trade keep getting younger. The conservative State-run press has printed articles on child prostitution, but it has usually focused on the problems in other countries. Nevertheless, the fact that it has printed any articles at all on this topic is significant. When the State-controlled press prints articles on a sensitive topic, it is usually because the issue has become a problem on the island. If the issue is not serious, the press tries to ignore it. Although Raul Castro's wife, Wilma Espin, the head of the Federation of Cuban Women and the closest thing Cuba has to a First Lady, has come out strongly against prostitution, the trade is thriving. The State has its crackdowns, but the *jineteras* just change location or disappear from the streets for a while, opting for the nightclubs.

Any young person seen with a foreigner runs the risk of being considered a *jinetera* or *jinetero*. A male American diplomat and a female Cuban employee of the U.S. Interests Section had an embarrassing moment when they went shopping together for a going-away present for a departing American. As they looked at merchandise in a store, the clerk tried to escort them into the lingerie department, because she assumed that the woman was a prostitute. A Cuban friend of mind made sure he had his identity papers with him whenever we went out together because, he said, "I don't want them to pick me up as a *jinetero!*"

To Have or Have Not

Beyond the realm of the worries of ordinary Cubans are the newly rich. They are conspicuous in their lifestyle and their consumption. The pounding bass from a powerful stereo in a Russian Lada driven by a young light-skinned Cuban is a prime example of the way the privileged young "haves" flaunt their wealth. With enough money to buy scarce and expensive gasoline, they entertain themselves drag racing on the road to the airport. They frequent the dollar nightclubs. They take their purebred Dobermans, dalmatians, and German shepherds to the dollar veterinarian where foreigners take their Cuban street mutts. The Castro government likes to present the self-employed as the newly rich, but while those people with their own enterprises do make up part of the nouveau riche, this class of conspicuous consumers is usually thought of by peso-earning Cubans as being comprised of the privileged children of high-level Party officials. As I strolled along First Avenue one evening with Agustin, a mulatto who earns pesos, he pointed out one newly restored building that was attracting a crowd for nightlife. He said, "Before the Revolution, that was a club for rich people. Do you know what it is now? A club for rich people." We walked further on and he pointed out another dramatic, handsome structure: "That used to be a club for rich people, too. Guess what it is now?"

The difference between having and not having is not a question of a television or new car. It is a difference of having meat, fruit, and vegetables or subsisting on rice and pork rinds; it is having cooking oil and soap, or doing without; it is driving a car instead of riding a bicycle in the rain. While for the "haves" the economic situation may be improving, for those who earn only pesos or receive only some dollars the outlook has not changed much. Because Cuban government economic statistics are less than reliable, to get a real measure of the economic climate, one must look at how people are living and what is happening on the streets. By the summer of 1996, it seemed that the State was almost ready to declare the Special Period over, thanks to economic growth and an influx of dollars. Gasoline was more available, and people had money to buy it, though usually at discounted black market prices. Many people could afford to visit the dollar stores and agricultural markets. Legal money exchange houses had been opened, so even those with peso salaries were able to obtain dollars and buy some necessities. The dollar continued to drop in value against the Cuban peso (many say because of State intervention), so the peso could buy more dollars and more goods. Unfortunately, prices were rising at the same time, canceling any potential gain. As a result, even though the streets were no longer empty of cars and shelves had been filled with food, the perceived living situation was just as bad as ever. In 1993, the goods were simply not there. Now that the goods were available, the prices were outrageous, far beyond the grasp of most Cubans. A bottle of cook-ing oil cost $2.75, and a small chicken cost at least $5.00. Expecta-tions had risen, but the economic and political realities were not keeping pace with the rising expectations.

While the separation between the haves and have-nots was no-ticeable from the time dollars were legalized, the difference was ex-acerbated by the goods and money brought by visiting relatives from the United States. From late 1995 through early 1996, as the link be-tween Cubans on the island and those outside strengthened, as fam-ilies were reunited, and as ideas and gifts were exchanged, the overall mood of the country improved. The nation seemed to be going for-ward; rumors of change were in the air. One of my friends, Marta Beatriz Roque, an independent economist who is now imprisoned, saw in this trend a great deal of hope. She perceived the visits and the influx of money to be causing social change. No longer were all, or even most, Cubans equal. Visiting relatives from the United States meant income, and the gulf between those with money and those without became more pronounced. This social change, she said, would have to yield economic and political change. It might have, except that the shooting down of two U.S.-based civilian aircraft by Cuban MiGs over the Straits of Florida in late February 1996 slammed the brakes on the opening. Since then, the gap between the haves and have-nots may have temporarily stabilized, but peo-ple remember the momentum that had been established. For many, the rising economic expectations and any accompanying political hopes are chafing against the reality Cubans are facing.

< 4 >

Varadero

Life for Tourists

Have you heard why lobster and shrimp have disappeared
from Cuba? They are carrying out an international socialist mission—
serving the tourists!
—a joke

On the road into Varadero, there is a large billboard with the words,
"Welcome to Varadero." I always thought they should add the message, "Now leaving Cuba." The Varadero beach resort is a tourist
haven and bears little resemblance to the rest of Cuba. In the large
tourist hotels, the only Cubans are the hotel workers and, of course,
the *jineteras*. The grounds are well groomed, the beaches are clean,
and waiters appear on the beach to serve anything from Coca-Cola
to rum drinks. Food and drink are abundant. Jet skis and catama-
rans are for rent. The sand is white and fine. The water is clear
turquoise. Varadero is a slice of paradise. Almost.

Not only in Varadero but throughout the island life for tourists
is completely different from life for Cubans. Vacationers have the
most privileged life in Cuba because they have dollars and can leave
whenever they choose. The tourist buses that cruise down the
Malecón hogging more than one lane are enclosed capsules from another world. Carefully insulated from contact with Cubans and the
difficulty of their lives, tourists are swept in air-conditioned luxury
from one exotic destination to another and then back to their hotels. Private yachts from many countries, including the United States,
sail into the Marina Hemingway to dock. Visitors pass their time at

the beach, sightseeing, or enjoying the charm and services of *jineteras.* Tourism is Fidel Castro's latest interest, and he has optimistic plans for attracting foreigners to his jewel of a Caribbean island. The national television news gives regular reports of new tourist establishments being built and speaks of the amenities to be offered to visitors. Unfortunately, few Cubans will ever see the inside of any of these hotels. All of this investment is for foreigners; it is being made to attract foreign currency. Cuban pesos cannot buy a cup of coffee at any of the hotels. Even if they have money, Cubans, except for prostitutes, are barred from entry by hotel doormen.

Tourists come mostly from Europe, Latin America, and Canada, since the U.S. government has long barred Americans from spending money in Cuba. People travel to the island for different reasons: Some come for the sun and beaches, some for the sex, some to see what the island is really like, and some in a show of socialist solidarity. There are few repeat visitors, however, because of the poor quality of service and food. Those who do return, mostly men, come not for the food or the beaches but for something more fundamental and female. The tourist industry is making an effort, but it does not have it quite right yet. While lavish buffets may be laid out, the previous night's vegetable might be offered as part of the breakfast spread.

The amount and variety of food on these buffets is, in the Cuban context, almost obscene. Fruit, eggs, cheese, cold cuts, cereal, yogurt, and any number of hot dishes appear for breakfast. Dinner yields shrimp, lobster, red snapper, turkey, and cornish hens. Imported kiwi fruit and strawberries grace a lunch buffet. An elaborate butter sculpture decorates the top of a buffet table in Varadero. And all of this opulence occurs in a country where mothers cannot get milk for children over seven years of age.

Even at the best hotels, service is poor because of insufficient training and incentive. Most of the workers are young, have never been off the island, and have no real understanding of how travelers expect to be treated. My experience at breakfast one Sunday in September 1996 at the five-star Meliá Cohiba serves as a good example. My table and those of two groups of Spanish tourists near us were covered with the previous occupants' dirty dishes. No one removed them until we were able to capture the attention of one of the few waiters. A well-dressed Spanish woman complained that her visit to Havana had been overpriced and marred by poor service. For the money she had spent, she could have gone to another island and received first-class treatment. After we waited about ten more minutes, it became clear that no one was going to offer coffee. Flagging down another waiter, I asked for coffee and queried him as to what was going on. He said, "There are not enough of us to take care of everyone." He added, "Several guests left without paying, and we [the employees] have to pay the missing money." At fifteen dollars a person, that would take a huge bite out of the Cubans' salaries and their desire to work.

The Hotel Nacional, with its twin turrets, is a Havana landmark. Famous people who have stayed there include Ed Bradley and Peter Jennings. High ceilings, tile floors, arched doorways, and expansive gardens combine to give the hotel an old-world elegance. But even the hotel's air of propriety cannot keep the reality of the outside economic conditions at bay. Quite apropos to Cuba's situation, "Tara's Theme" from *Gone With the Wind* sometimes plays over the sound system. Shortly after my arrival on the island, as I waited in the lobby to meet an incoming American delegation, it did not take me long to become thankful that I had dressed in a conservative blouse and long skirt. All of the other single women in the lobby were for hire, and some of the men were looking at me as if I were as well. Two of the young women who strolled through had dyed their hair blond and were wearing brightly colored spandex, but most of the ladies working the Nacional were dressed for more discerning customers. One of these women could have been a statuesque well-dressed Latina going out for the evening had she not been wearing black lace stockings with her very short black dress. Her attire and deferential attitude toward the portly European at her side left little doubt about her status. Sadly, she was probably university educated and may have been someone's mother. Although ordinary Cubans are not allowed into the hotel or gardens, they can enjoy one part of the Nacional. The quiet garden of the hotel reaches almost to the Malecón and offers one of the best views of the sea and Havana. The ground drops sharply not far from there, and at the corner of the grounds, there is a waterfall that cascades into a refreshing fountain pool on the Malecón. When the weather is warm, local children play in that fountain, with their mothers watching over them.

Cuba is famous for innovative music and impressive floor shows, but most of these performances are priced so expensively in dollars that few people besides tourists and other foreigners can afford to enjoy them. The Hotel Riviera, which before the Revolution was a glamorous locale that attracted movie stars, is now the home of the Palacio de la Salsa, where the island's best salsa bands play. The Riviera's decor has changed little since the 1950s, and that is part of the hotel's charm. For Cubans who earn pesos, an evening at the Palacio de la Salsa is out of reach because the cover charge is so high. One Thursday evening a visiting friend and I invited a Cuban couple, Jaime and Carolina, to join us for dancing. Jaime said the best music would be at the Palacio, so we went there. The couple had not been to the club since their honeymoon years before. My friend paid the ten-dollar cover charge for each of us, but Jaime was a bit embarrassed: "It costs my entire month's salary to come in here," he said. "I would never have suggested this place if I had known it was this expensive." We danced the night away, sipped our five-dollar Mojitos (a Cuban rum drink with lime and mint), and listened to Rojitas y su Grupo perform salsa music. My friends told me they had not enjoyed an evening like that in years.

Another must-see for visitors to Havana is the extravagant floor show at the Tropicana. In this time capsule from the 1950s, it is not surprising that some of the valet parking attendants have been working there—doing the same job—since before the Revolution. The park-like setting places a distance between the patron and the outside world. Before performances, visitors can stroll through a jungle-like garden or dine at an elegant restaurant. Once all the visitors have paid for their thirty-dollar seats and made their way to the tables arranged around the open-air stage, the lights go down and the timeless spectacle begins. On a platform high in the canopy of trees, talented singers perform their lively accompaniment to the parade of dancers and the elaborate show that unfolds on the expansive open-air stage. As a man sings, dancers in brief silver costumes topped off with chandelier headdresses fill the stage. Electricity is carried to the chandeliers by a cord that runs from one woman to the next. In another moment, women in tiny bikinis and feather headdresses strut across the stage and down the aisles, pausing to dance in front of spectators' tables. My companion was so stunned when a dancer stopped just a foot from our table that he did not notice that the woman was wearing fishnet stockings—I think he was captivated by what she was not wearing.

During the day, for tourists interested in handicrafts, there is the *feria* (fair) on the Malecón. It is an *artesanía* (handicraft) market, but the locals call it a fair because anything called a market would sound like capitalism and raise suspicion. At the *feria,* vendors sell, for dollars and pesos, simple foodstuffs, handmade shoes, wood carvings, ceramics, old books, and American baseball cards. (Mickey Mantle, anyone?) Cuba does not have a tradition of handicrafts. These artisans are likely to be out-of-work university-educated people who have discovered that they can make a better living selling crafts created with poor quality materials for dollars than they can working in an office where they earn peso salaries.

The Plaza de la Catedral is another place where vendors hawk their wares to tourists. Visitors also get a bit of local color there. Children and adults beg for coins. Live music pours from a restaurant on the square. Necklaces, dolls, paintings, and knickknacks are for sale. An enterprising representative of a nearby *paladar* tries to lure foreigners to his restaurant while regaling them in English with stories of his time living in New York before the Cuban Revolution. For the artistically inclined, the Galeria Wilfredo Lam is just around the corner, and there is a studio for making artistic lithographs at the far end of the square. Speaking Spanish adds another dimension to the experience, making the visitor privy to some interesting comments. In one exchange, I heard young men admiring female tourists and one speculating whether he could "get a girlfriend like that to take him out of the country." About a block away is Bodeguita del Medio, rumored to have been one of Ernest Hemingway's favorite haunts.

Not far away, a visitor can get an education about the Revolution and its propaganda by visiting the Museo de la Revolución. A colleague of mine called it "ground zero" for the next revolution. This elaborate baroque-style building was once the presidential palace. Within it, one can find clothing worn by Raul Castro, bloodstained shirts worn by martyrs of the Revolution, and life-size sculptures of Che Guevara and Camilo Cienfuegos. Reading the statements about life before the Revolution was most revealing and must give Cubans pause. One reads: "Before the Revolution, many women were forced into prostitution because of the economic situation." A bit farther on, I saw: "Families went hungry before the Revolution."

The site of the "first defeat of American imperialism in Latin America"—Playa Giron, better known to Americans as the Bay of Pigs—is a popular tourist destination because of the quality scuba diving. Along the road to Playa Giron are markers for the fallen dead from the invasion. The museum that commemorates the event boasts a Cuban military airplane that flew in 1961 and the fuselage of an American plane downed during the conflict. Belongings of the fallen from both sides are displayed along with photos, letters, and other memorabilia. One item on display, found on a fallen Cuban was a small satchel made out of U.S. Army green canvas with the letters "U.S." stenciled in black. When I asked the museum attendant what the initials stood for, she said "Union Sovietica" (Soviet Union). Of course.

The land en route to Playa Giron is swampy and covered with dense vegetation. There is an alligator preserve not far from the bay, and the area has a variety of birds and other wildlife. At certain times of the year there are so many crabs crossing the road that vehicles often get flat tires from the pointed claws and breaking shells. On the road to the beaches near Playa Giron, tourists may find themselves behind a truck full of Cubans going to the beach. The Cuban government often sponsors trips to the beach as a reward to a workplace. The transportation provided, however, is hardly elegant. The shipment of people in trucks like cargo is common all over the island. On the way to the beach, I saw a number of one-and-a-half-ton 1950s vintage American trucks with their open beds loaded with about fifty people, young and old, male and female. The Cubans were not bound for the same beach, however, as foreigners were. The State prefers to have locals and visitors separated.

The second time I went to Playa Giron, I traveled with the political counselor of the U.S. Interests Section, one of the Marines, and his visiting girlfriend. As members of the Interests Section, we had to file a form with the Foreign Ministry five working days in advance in order to travel outside the city limits of Havana. We left Havana early one Saturday and by midmorning were snorkeling and diving in Caleta Buena, a delightful and unexploited cove protected by a coral reef. Drawn to the clear blue water and white coral, I left my towel on a chair under a palm-thatched cabana, climbed down a ladder, and found myself in warm, beautiful, waist-deep water. A short swim away was a reef teeming with life. After lunch, we made a short drive to a nearby *cenote,* a fresh-water hole that somewhere, eighty meters below, connected to the ocean. In the *cenote*, cold fresh and salt water mixed in a filmy layer, and fish as exotic as those darting around the reef presented themselves. Later in the afternoon, we walked across the street to the ocean, planning to go in the water, but two official Cubans stopped us and several Russian and German tourists. One man in uniform and another in plain clothes with a sidearm said we were not allowed to go scuba diving because the military would be having exercises. I engaged the plainclothes officer in conversation, asking if we could at least go snorkeling. He said, "No. No snorkeling and no diving because of the military exercises." Then he said, "You are Cati, right?" I asked him how he knew my name was Cati, and he responded, "You just look like a Cati." Nothing like being incognito.

The unspoiled beaches of the island are some of the favorite destinations of foreigners resident in Cuba. These beaches are not as accessible as those of Varadero, so few tourists find them. For those of us who were not tourists, the unspoiled beaches gave us a bit of peace, an escape. It is not easy being "the enemy." At the beach we could relax. One Sunday, a group of about ten of us went to a beach called Herradura, about an hour west of Havana. The narrow rutted lane that connects the main road to the beach winds through a cane field. After we had set up our towels and coolers on the beach, a white Lada, with a family inside, parked next to us. By the time the beach crowd thinned and we began grilling our hamburgers, it became obvious that these were not average beachgoers parked next to us. That evening, a certain tranquillity settled over our group as we sat on the beach and watched the sun set and later the moon rise. We had never stayed at the beach that long, but we felt as if we had escaped for a while, and no one wanted the moment to end. We could tell that our watchers in the Lada were getting a bit restless. They must have been wondering if we were ever going to leave. I am sure the kids wanted to go home. I hope daddy got overtime.

The cannon firing at nine o'clock in the evening is one of the best attractions Havana has to offer. It is a joy, partly because Cubans, who pay only three pesos, and foreigners mix easily for the show. At almost all the other sites, there is little or no interaction (except for the money-making variety) between tourists and local people. Every evening, "soldiers" at *El Morro*, a fortress completed in 1630 that overlooks Havana's harbor, reenact the cannon firing of colonial times. Originally, the shot was fired each night to announce the raising of a heavy chain across the harbor to keep out unwelcome ships. Wooden sailing ships trying to come in under the cover of darkness would have seriously damaged their hulls on the chain. Today, as silence falls on crowds gathered on the lawn, two young men dressed in white light torches to illuminate the scene. Then a procession of young men wearing colonial Spanish uniforms and carrying period weapons emerges from the fortress. They present their arms and proceed through the ceremony, entrancing the audience. It is only when the cannon explodes with sound and the soldiers march away that the spell is broken and the twentieth century descends again.

< 5 >

Triumphs of the Revolution

Health Care and Education

The accomplishments of Fidel's regime are referred to as triumphs of the Revolution. The provision of universal health care and the guarantee of education for all are probably the two most widely celebrated of these achievements. Cuba currently boasts the lowest infant mortality rate in Latin America and the second highest literacy rate, lagging behind only Argentina. A little noted fact is that in 1957, according to United Nations data, the island also had the lowest infant mortality rate. While the literacy rate has improved from 76 to 96 percent since 1957, improving Cuba's ranking in the region from fourth to second in this area, the nation's achievement has been surpassed by Paraguay and Colombia. Both of those countries have registered larger percentage gains in literacy, bringing rates from 68 and 62 percent, respectively, all the way up to 92 and 91 percent in 1995. Although the Castro government has a need to stress its successes, especially during the economic crisis it faces, the reality is that health care in general has deteriorated markedly during the Special Period and having an educated populace can make it difficult to control the flow of ideas and maintain the regime.

Health Care

The news on the health care system at first glance appears to be good. Fidel Castro lauds the advances medical research teams have made in developing new vaccines and surgical techniques. Television reports declare that the nation has so many trained doctors that it is exporting them to South Africa and other countries to work in rural areas. Indeed, patients come from all parts of the world to Cuba for medical treatment, even though there is doubt as to whether some of the treatments are effective.

Average Cubans see the truth behind the facade. Although Fidel says that not a single hospital has closed since the Special Period began, people know the hospitals are not in good shape. Physical facilities have not been kept up, creating unpleasant, if not unsanitary, results. For example, one hospital's maternity ward had a bathroom that contained a toilet, but it had no seat and did not flush. The shower consisted of a rusty pipe sticking out of the wall. Below the pipe, the wall was stained and filthy. It is not merely fixtures that are lacking, as I learned soon after a friend named Lucrecia, who had been laid off from her job in printing because there was no paper, landed a job as the head of a cleaning crew at a hospital. When I saw her a week after she began her new job, her euphoria over being employed had turned to disgust. She had quit her job. She told me, "There was no soap or disinfecting solution. There were no cleaning rags. How can anyone clean when there is nothing to clean with?"

Because of the difficulty of disinfecting hospitals, infections are common after surgery and childbirth. After a Cuban colleague's wife gave birth to a little girl, I asked about the mother and baby. "The baby is doing very well," the thin twenty-eight-year-old said, "but my wife has an infection. I just found out that the hospital has a big problem with infections. If I had known, I would never have let her go to that maternity ward. I go there now on my bicycle twice a day to take her food. *No es fácil.*"

Another problem for many Cubans is finding transportation to the hospital. The experience of Lizette, a young, recently married woman who lived in the apartment building next door to my house, was all too common. Lizette would strike up conversations with me, usually about the cats that lived in my yard and helped mouse hers. One day she excitedly told me that she was pregnant. When she was at about the six-month point, she came to my door panicked because she thought she was going to miscarry. I took her to the clinic in my car. As it turned out, she was fine. As her due date approached, Lizette knew I could not drive her anywhere because my car was not running. Lizette's mother explained to me that she had saved and purchased five dollars' worth of gasoline to give to a neighbor to drive her to the hospital. When the time came, neither of the owners of the two cars on our block were available. I called a taxi for them and paid in dollars for their trip.

Lizette delivered a little girl. The newborn slept in a large dark blue baby carriage that had probably been around since the 1950s. Her diapers were not diapers, but layers of hospital gauze, which would be washed until the material fell apart. The gauze had been stolen from the hospital and sold on the black market. When the baby was a few months old, Lizette started crushing eggshells to mix with water to feed her baby. They were the child's source of calcium.

While people have access, however difficult, to medical care, they do not necessarily have access to medicine. Doctors give prescriptions, but the drugs are not available for pesos and at times are not available for dollars either. I learned this firsthand when my arm was fractured and the orthopedist prescribed a painkiller. When I tried to obtain it, I found the hospital dollar pharmacy did not have it.

Even if dollar pharmacies have medicine in stock, this does not help the Cubans, because these stores are reserved only for foreigners. At one of these, an Angolan diplomat was in line behind a Cuban who wanted to purchase asthma medicine for her daughter. The woman asked for the medicine, but the pharmacist would not give it to her, even though the medicine was available. The woman put her dollars on the counter, but the pharmacist still would not sell it to her. The Angolan asked what was wrong, because he knew the woman had the dollars to pay. The woman was Cuban and, therefore, was not allowed to purchase the medicine for her daughter. The Angolan bought the medicine for her, he said, "Because I am a

Christian." For those who have no dollars, there are only two choices: doing without or buying on the black market.

An independent journalist who visited my office one day was grimacing with pain because he had broken his hand the day before. The hand had been wrapped by a doctor, but no painkiller had been available. It is not just prescription drugs that are hard to come by; even a bottle of aspirin is a rare commodity. Most Cubans who have aspirin received it from family visiting from the States. In this strange health care environment, a visiting foreigner can have specialized surgery and care, but a Cuban cannot get an aspirin for a headache. In Santiago de Cuba, an elderly professional woman with two fractured vertebrae was delighted to receive aspirin and a few painkillers from visitors. "I hate going to the doctor," she said. "It is a long way there, and I have to walk. If he prescribes something, I don't know if I will be able to get it. The pharmacy near me rarely has anything, so I have to go across town."

Nutrition, or rather the lack of it, is also causing health problems. In the worst days of the Special Period, neuritis caused by vitamin deficiencies became a problem. Many of those afflicted were women who were the heads of extended families. They had been eating very poorly, preferring to give the limited food to their children and grandchildren. In September 1996, the Communist Party daily, *Granma,* ran an article announcing that there had been over one hundred cases of neuritis reported in Cuba and that special vitamins were now available for five pesos. An academic accustomed to reading between the lines noted, "If they say there have been one hundred cases, there have been at least two hundred." The stress of the daily battle for survival compounds the nutrition problem. High blood pressure and migraines are common. Doctors gave special diets to two women I know who were suffering from high blood pressure. They both complained that it was almost impossible to go on a special diet in Cuba. "How am I supposed to eat vegetables?" they said. "Do you know how much they cost?" Rice, beans, and pork rinds hardly make a healthy diet.

Deteriorating sanitary conditions are not helping to improve the health of Cubans. At a birthday party I ran into Anita, an elegant, gray-haired, fifty-five-year-old woman who lives in Centro Habana. She was wearing sandals and her big toe was bandaged. "What happened?" I asked. To that question, she gave a disturbing answer:

> I was bitten by a rat. When I walked into my living room this morning, there was a ten-inch-long rat under the sofa. The rat was too big for the dog, so I tried to get him out the door. The rat took off and ran up the wall. I was chasing him all over, and then he turned on me and bit my toe. I knew I had to get medical attention—for heaven's sake, I had been bitten by a rat. I went to the clinic in my neighborhood to get a shot or some kind of treatment. They told me they did not have a vaccine and could do nothing for me, so I should see my family doctor. I went to my family doctor and he said, "Can you describe the rat?"
>
> "Well," I said, "he was gray and about ten inches long."
>
> "The coat was all the same?"
>
> "Yes, the coat was smooth."
>
> "How was he moving?"
>
> "Oh," I said, "he was moving quickly."
>
> "So, you are saying the rat seemed healthy?"
>
> "Well, yes, he seemed to be healthy."
>
> "Okay, I can't do anything for you. Go home and don't worry about it."

Rats are a problem throughout Cuba. Leptospirosis, a disease associated with contact with rat feces, is on the rise. An article in the labor union newspaper, *Trabajadores,* acknowledged the increase in cases and encouraged people to use the new vaccine biotechnology researchers had developed. After discussing the vaccine for two-thirds of the article, the journalist recommended that people wash their hands thoroughly, and finally, in the last paragraph, he said that the best way to avoid leptospirosis is to control the rat population and have regular garbage collection. This service, however, deteriorated markedly as garbage trucks broke down and could not be fixed. In Miramar, my neighborhood, dumpsters were often filled to capacity, but they were emptied fairly regularly, partly because so many foreigners paid top dollar rent to live in restored houses in the area. When the garbage was not collected, a pile would accumulate on the corner that was two to three feet high and stretched for about thirty feet. In the downtown neighborhoods of Centro Habana and Havana Vieja the situation was worse, and in other areas the State had stopped providing garbage collection altogether. I was visiting independent economist Marta Beatriz Roque at her home in the neighborhood of Santo Suarez one afternoon when two men in their mid-twenties came to her door. She gave them a few pesos. The men, one dark-skinned and one light-skinned, were Jehovah's Witnesses who could not find employment with the State. They collect the garbage in Santo Suarez, a job no one else wants to do and a service the regime is no longer able to offer. Through an agreement with the government, these young men were collecting the garbage and then, once a month, going door-to-door to collect a few pesos for their work. The Cubans are annoyed that the State is not providing this basic service. One *paladar* employee summed it up with, "Let's see if these *communists* can manage to pick up the garbage by September 28 [the next holiday]."

The evening I chatted with the woman with the rat bite, I spoke with a number of other fifty- to sixty-year-old women. They had laughed with Anita about the rat bite, because if they had not they would have cried. They had all dealt with rats in their homes. For home medical cures, they were using their grandmothers' and great grandmothers' remedies. "After all," one commented, "we are living like they did." The Revolution's triumph of providing health care is falling apart as the State is proving itself unable to preserve basic levels of nutrition and public health necessities like garbage collection.

Education

Education is another commonly heralded triumph of the Revolution. Cubans are tremendously well educated and capable. Once they have the chance to exist without the weight of an oppressive State, they should be able to shape their own future and make their own way in the world. Even working within the political and economic constraints placed upon them, they have achieved a great deal. They are conducting newsworthy scientific and medical research. Language teachers are excellent. Musicians and dancers are world class. Using their minds, force of will, and very limited basic resources, Cubans work miracles. One visiting American museum expert commented, "Last year, two Cubans visited our museum to participate in a workshop. I doubt if the American participants implemented any of the ideas we addressed; they would have said they did not have the money or the resources. The Cubans, on the other hand, took what they had learned, modified it to suit their needs, and implemented a cataloging procedure for their museum—and they did it with almost no resources. These people are amazing."

Unfortunately, education in a society that does not have the basic freedom of expression is a double-edged sword. One of the saddest elements of life in Cuba today is that there are thousands of educated thinkers held prisoner in their own minds—a hellish internal prison. What value is knowing how to write if one's hands are tied? What use is knowing how to read if every word is filtered by the government before it is seen? What use is thinking when there is no outlet for new ideas? Cubans know that free expression of ideas leads down a narrow path to prison or exile. There is no place for intellectuals on this island. Thinking people are a threat to any intolerant regime. The Castro government would prefer to minimize the influence of new ideas by exposing its people only to the views it promulgates. But in this age of mass communication, complete isolation is difficult to attain. Miami and Key West radio stations can be received on the island, and short-wave radio brings in the entire world. While it is nearly impossible to stop all the voices that reach the island on the airwaves, the regime has strictly limited the importation of books, newspapers, and magazines. Nevertheless, despite the State's efforts to impede the flow of information from the outside world, ideas, ultimately, have a life of their own.

For many Cubans, intellectual integrity is a source of heartache. Because of the strict adherence to the Party line required by the regime, social science academics, for example, are seriously limited in the work they can do. Several years ago, Miriam Gras, a professor of political science and U.S. specialist at the University of Havana and a Communist Party member, wrote an academic paper for a conference on the island in which she argued that to achieve the goals of the Revolution, the Party had to be reformed. When part of the paper was published in the *Miami Herald,* Miriam found herself thrown out of the Party. She stayed on as a university professor but was ostracized by many of her colleagues. When I last saw her, she had been thrown out of the university for her views.

For students, as well, the question of intellectual integrity arises. Diana, a twenty-year-old university student with fair skin and big brown eyes who lived with her grandmother, told me she had been studying law but left the department even though it meant she would have to retake entrance exams and would lose credit for a year of course work. "We had been studying the law and learning that a person is innocent until proven guilty," she said. "Then they took us to view a trial. The person was considered guilty just because he was brought to trial. That is not the rule of law. I am studying accounting now. I don't think they can make accounting political."

Artists, dancers, and musicians are given a bit more leeway because they do not use words and their messages are less direct. Only one prominent artist, Jose Angel Toirac, actually creates images of Fidel Castro. When he was invited to exhibit in Miami, he planned to replace Fidel's image with that of his wife, since paintings of the leader are not to leave the country. The messages of most paintings are more subtle. One young hearing-impaired artist paints street scenes exactly as he sees them. One included a water truck providing potable water, two policemen sharing one bicycle, and a policeman asking for a *jinetera*'s papers. Pedro Baldriche paints the city with an architect's eye; he paints in gray but then, unexpectedly, places a shining gold pyramid on a city corner. "Everywhere," he told me, "you see the run-down buildings; then you come to a building that has to do with dollars." Another theme of this artist's work is a wall with spikes on top. The wall has some cracks near the top, but it is foreboding. On the other side of the wall lies welcoming blue water. The wall reflects a sentiment expressed by one intellectual who commented, "The island is the most beautiful prison on earth."

Even though artists work without words, they, like other intellectuals, must limit their ideas and practice self-censorship. Adding to the frustration for many is the difficulty in obtaining art supplies. One artist, tired of having to struggle simply to eat every day, said, "I do not feel that I am alive. I cannot feel; I cannot love—not the way I want to. I need to be free." People can withstand many hardships, but restrictions on thought may be the most draining. Roberto, the musician in Santiago de Cuba, commented, "There are some good things that have come from the Revolution. And now we are getting by economically. People like [National Assembly President] Ricardo Alarcon and [Vice President] Carlos Lage are making good decisions. But what we need, what we all want, is more freedom."

‹ 6 ›

Civil Society

Before the Revolution, there was a fully developed civil society on the island. Professional associations, fraternal organizations, and social clubs were thriving. A walk through the main cemetery in Santiago de Cuba or Havana serves as a reminder of how active citizens once were, as tombstones are engraved with the names or symbols of organizations, such as the Masons, to which the people once belonged. The State, which did not want to see people come together for any reason other than the glory of the Revolution, wiped out almost all of these civic groups, replacing them with socialist ones, from the Young Pioneers to the Federation of Cuban Women. The government still does not want independent organizations to exist, because they would threaten the State. Cubans are not allowed to meet in groups without the blessing of the regime, and they can be charged with illegal association if they do. If people were permitted to meet in groups, they might be able to organize and create a real opposition to Fidel Castro.* The State claims that Cuba has all the civic organizations it needs with the Federation of Cuban Women, the Union of Young Communists, the Federation of University Students, and other related State organizations. A number of Cubans would disagree.

If people wish to form an organization, they must ask the permission of the State. One group of motorcycle aficionados wanted to be recognized. Although most of them preferred their treasured

---

* On a related note, when it appeared that nongovernmental organizations might be able to obtain access to foreign funds, the Cuban government started disguising some of its think tanks, and even the Committees for the Defense of the Revolution, as nongovernmental organizations, even though they are clearly government-organized institutions.

antique Harley Davidsons, they included anyone in the group who owned a vintage motorcycle. The government declined their petition. Another group of people interested in yoga and Indian culture tried to be recognized. They were denied and told to join a State organization for friendship between peoples. They dropped the idea. In the former Soviet Union, the environment was one of the first issues around which independent organizations were allowed to develop. After all, how can the government be opposed to protecting the environment? Several nongovernmental environmental groups have so far successfully formed in Cuba, and only one seems to be government organized. The others are made up of scientists and ecologists who specifically avoid politics. Many of the individuals running these nongovernmental organizations (NGOs) are scientists with doctorates earned at universities abroad. They work within the system and have contact with their counterparts in the United States. Though they may raise the suspicions of the State, they carefully comply with the regulations. They have found their niche and are doing all they can from the foothold they have carved.

The Masons

The most significant NGO in Cuba, besides the Catholic church, is the fraternal organization of the Masons. The Masons have survived, despite going through hard times. Their lodges, which exist in almost every town, stand as eloquent reminders of a world that was. The Grand Masonic Lodge opened with great pageantry in 1958. It is a landmark, standing on the corner of what once were important commercial streets. The clock on the building has ceased to function, and the walls of the top floor are so weathered and crumbling that sunlight peeks through some small holes. High above, on top of the building, the Masonic symbol and a globe are reminders that this land has not always belonged to Fidel.

Although many Cuban Masons left for the United States at the beginning of the Revolution, a good number stayed and kept the fraternal organization alive. There are now some 20,000 Masons on the island, and the group continues to grow. That the organization is gaining strength is exceptional considering the restrictions the regime places on association and the significant political role that members of the organization have played in the island's history. Masons proudly claim, for example, that two champions of Cuban independence, José Martí and Antonio Maceo, were members of the brotherhood. The group has a tradition of mutual support, but now it is trying to revive some of its traditional charitable activities as well. In 1996 the organization asked permission from the State to help supply school uniforms to needy families. That permission was denied. Members of this group are very proud to be Cubans, but they also respect and are loyal to their Masonic brothers worldwide. They recognize their strong and historic tie to the United States and will eagerly point out prominent American historical figures who were Masons. Perhaps because of this connection, they have been willing to have contact with the U.S. Interests Section.

The beginning of my relationship with the Grand Masonic Lodge was the day Lucrecia Marrero, the number-two person in the women's equivalent of the Masons, the Hijas de Acacia, bustled into the USIS office with exciting news. Lucrecia is a plump, blond, bubbly ball of energy who radiates enthusiasm. She had just received permission from the State organization that oversees Masonic activities to hang an exhibit of posters from the New York School of Design that USIS had offered. The restrictions were that we had ten days to put up the exhibit, we could not publicize it, and we could display it for only one week. Although art exhibits are usually planned well in advance and publicized, we were excited about the opportunity. Given the difficult environment of U.S.-Cuba relations, it seemed to be evidence that miracles do occur. This was the first U.S.-sponsored exhibit on the island since the Revolution.

When I saw the exhibit space, I realized that we had a tremendous amount of work to do. We had a room but no usable wall space.

Since the State had allowed the art show, we decided to try renting some exhibit stands from a government institution. A gentleman checked and measured the space, gave an estimate, and then, less than forty-eight hours before the exhibit was to open, backed out and said he could not supply the stands. He had stopped by the Ministry of Foreign Relations the day he measured the space, and officials there had probably told him not to rent the stands to us at any price. Although I had been in Havana for only four months, I was not surprised. Still, I knew we would pull it off. I knew Cubans had a way of making things work.

Three members of the local USIS staff (who, I discovered, could do virtually anything), a group of Masons and I scrounged for wood, paint, and other necessary materials and then designed and built free-standing walls on which to hang the framed posters. The night before the exhibit was to open, a group of us worked late into the night. The head of the Masonic group that evening was Orlando Gonzalez, the grand secretary of the Masons and Lucrecia's husband. Orlando is a thin man with a polite manner and a strong sense of honor who had worked as a carpenter most of his adult life. He was a former political prisoner and had not been allowed to return to his profession as a teacher when he was released from prison. Working with these people, hammering, sawing, painting, and designing with enthusiasm until nearly midnight, showed me what Cubans can achieve when they have a goal.

During that busy week of preparation, Lucrecia asked me if USIS could lend a tape of the U.S. national anthem and a U.S. flag. She wanted to use these in the opening ceremony. I explained that the Cuban government did not permit us to display the flag outdoors or to play the national anthem. I also told her it was probably not advisable for the Masons to do that either. The night of the art opening, she told me she had a surprise for me. Lo and behold, she had found a forty-eight starred American flag and had displayed it alongside the Cuban one. At the beginning of the festivities, a tape of the

Cuban anthem was played, followed by a rendition of "The Star Spangled Banner." Lucrecia beamed at me, showing her delight that she had been able to create a ceremony that honored both nations. During the course of the week, several hundred people passed through the exhibit, leaving comments in a guest book that ranged from an art student's "*Genial!*" ("Cool!") to a José Martí quote that read, "*Ser culto es la unica manera de ser libre*" ("To be cultured is the only way to be free").

The Masonic library was watched over by Gustavo Pardo, a former political prisoner and self-taught historian who loves to talk. He has laughing eyes and a manner that belies the difficult road he has traveled. He was like a proud father as he escorted people through the library and explained the treasures held there. There are, he told me, books and materials in the library from Cuba's history that neither the National Archives nor the National Library hold. Added to those treasures were literally thousands of books donated by Masons who left the country at the beginning of the Revolution. He asked eagerly if we could give him books to update the collection, and USIS gladly complied, giving him multiple copies of books to add to the Mason's lending library. The volumes on politics, history, economics, and environmental issues donated by our office were displayed alongside books on Marxism.

All good things come to an end, or at least they do in Castro's Cuba. State Security officials appeared at the Grand Masonic Lodge in August 1996 demanding access to the library. They went in and immediately rooted out some books that the government considered objectionable. The officials demanded that Gustavo Pardo be removed from his position and replaced with a Mason they named— someone unknown to the organization's hierarchy. State Security then removed all of the books that USIS had given to the library, which ranged in subject from baseball to the environment to politics to biographies to free-market economics. In addition, the officials demanded that Pardo be tried before the Masonic court for having brought these "subversive" materials into the lodge. If the requests of the State were not met, the fraternal organization would lose the library and might be shut down altogether. The Masons were given no choice.

Lucrecia and Orlando are now living in the United States with their two children. They were approved as political refugees because of Orlando's time as a political prisoner at the beginning of the Revolution and because of the harassment that began against them about the time of the art exhibit. When Lucrecia told me they needed to leave the island, I felt like I had been punched in the stomach. I had not realized how heavily State persecution had fallen upon them in the wake of the art show. When I saw Orlando, he was wan and drawn, his skin pallid. He was a far cry from the energetic man with whom I had worked to present that art exhibit. He had never wanted to leave Cuba, and he is a patriot, but the harassment had reached such a level that he saw no other way. He was afraid the State was going to send him to prison, and with his sixtieth birthday only weeks away, he did not think he would survive. Once they were approved as refugees and knew they would be leaving, it was as if the cloud of oppression over them had disappeared. They had hope, and they had a future. They arrived in Colorado, their resettlement site, in January 1997. Though they arrived in a snowstorm, a group of Cuban Americans braved the weather to meet them at the airport. Lucrecia, Orlando, and their children are happily settling into a new life and a brighter future.

< 7 >

Why Don't They Rise Up?

With all the hardship Cubans face, the question outsiders always have is, "Why don't they rebel?" Although rebellion seems like a step Cubans would take, the reality is that people will withstand great hardship when they believe they cannot change their situation. At present, many barriers, including the pervasive presence of State Security, the culture of mistrust, and the fear of change, discourage Cubans from overtly challenging authority. They must decide they want change and be willing to act to bring about that change. People know what they are risking and do not want to take on a quixotic challenge. They have seen that dissent seems to have little impact on the system but has a great deal of negative impact on the one dissenting. When I spoke of Aung San Suu Kyi (the famous Burmese human rights activist) and quoted a message she had for people in oppressed countries, a professional woman who has two daughters said, "She is one in a million. Only one in a million people could do that. I could not. I do not want to be a martyr." How can you rise up when you believe you will be put down?

Teresa, a dark-haired woman in her late fifties who as a university student had fought in the streets against then-President Batista, said, "I thought life under Batista was bad, but that is nothing compared to this. You cannot move in this country." This "inability to move" is the result of the stranglehold State Security has on the Cuban people. Because of the sense that someone is always watching or listening, individuals are afraid to say or do anything that might be considered counterrevolutionary. Speaking out against the State can mean hunger or much worse. If individual Cubans could get past the barrier of fear and begin to organize, they would be impeded by the State because of laws against "illicit association." But perhaps more daunting would be the obstacles resulting from the culture of

mistrust that has developed. Because individuals have learned to suspect others and their motivations, it would be hard for a group to
develop the level of trust needed to organize effectively. If, indeed,
people were to organize, where would they find a leader? The only
prominent figure in Cuba besides Fidel is the Catholic cardinal,
Jaime Ortega, an unlikely candidate for political leadership. Over
the years, Fidel has removed anyone who could develop a following.
He does not want an internal opposition. He wants no voices save
his own. He will brook no competition. He never has. He can ele-
vate Che Guevara and Camilo Cienfuegos to high status, because
there is nothing like a dead hero.

Despite the jarring difficulties of daily life and the constant trauma
of performing a political high-wire act, people fear change. Even
though they know their situation is bad right now, they are afraid it
will be worse if the system changes. They have a sense of economic
security now that they want to preserve. There may not be aspirin
in the hospitals, but they know they have guaranteed medical care.
They may not be well paid at their jobs, but they fear that if change
comes and all the capitalist influence of the Miami Cuban community rushes in, they will lose their jobs, their homes, and their futures—however tenuous those futures may be. The idea of living
like Americans, paying high rent and insurance, and having no safety
net is truly frightening. One very talented man who speaks beautiful English and should never have a problem finding a job expressed
his anxiety by asking, "What will happen to us? What will happen
to me when change comes? We will lose everything. We will lose our
jobs. What will we do?" The owner of a *paladar* said that she welcomed change, but when asked how she felt about the idea of competition from foreign businesses, she admitted she was not yet ready
for that kind of challenge. Years of indoctrination have made Cubans
anxious about their future. Even though they are beaten down and
suffering, they have been convinced that everything will be worse if
they throw Fidel out. Cubans are concerned that the coming of

change means that the "mafiosos from Miami," whom the State press vilifies daily, will descend upon the island. They believe those who left Cuba will return and try to turn back the hands of time to the "neocolonial era."

Maritza, a lively professor with short red hair, explained the situation like this: "People realize they are in a box they cannot leave. There is no way out. So they convince themselves that the box is a really nice place to be. They tell themselves the world outside the box is a bad place. The box is safe and good. This message is drilled into their heads every day as they watch the news and television programs. The news from Cuba is good. The news from the rest of the world is almost uniformly bad. If someone dares to say life in the box is not good, the person is rebuffed and ridiculed. Life in the box has to be protected and preserved because there is too much at stake for the box to be damaged." The Cubans are afraid of losing what they have. They may not have much, but they know food, education, and health care are guaranteed. They do not know what change will bring. So they wait. They wait for an opportunity or for Fidel's death.

Castro's political system is static, contradicting Chinese Communist leader Mao Zedong's assertion that "red is the color of constant revolution." Cuba, though, is changing, and the Revolution must evolve with it if it is to survive. However, Fidel refuses to allow such evolution, so tension is building. A professor I know acknowledged the strangled state of life and then added, "He [Fidel] has made it clear that there is no way to change the system from within and there is no way to change it from outside. Because of that, there is only one way out." Teresa, the woman mentioned earlier who fought against Batista, gave a name to that way out when she stated with pain in her voice, "There will be bloodshed. There is so much hate. There will be bloodshed, and it is coming soon." The people have been oppressed and deprived for too long for them to go peacefully into any transition.

In the past few years, people have been struggling to feed themselves and their families. It is hard to think about politics when one is worried about survival. Now, despite the ongoing difficulties, people are a little better off, thanks to either money from relatives or a slightly healthier local economy. With a little food in their stomachs, they can think about the situation in their country. Outbreaks of leptospirosis, the lack of garbage pickup, and the unavailability of school uniforms are more pieces of kindling on a fire that is set to burn. People are angry, and that anger is manifesting itself within families; people are fighting with one another at home—the one place where it has always been essential to stand together for survival. At times, it seems that all it would take for violence to flare is a match.

With tears in her eyes, a woman who works for the State declared, "I don't know why Fidel hates us so much. Why does he just keep trying to crush us? We believed in the Revolution. We supported him and brought him to power. Now what do we have? *No es fácil. No es fácil.* My children have nothing to hope for. They deserve better than this. They just want to leave. Why does he keep going back on his word? This cannot go on, or we will have a civil war." Even a loyal member of the Party admitted, "I have never felt this way before, despite all we have been through. I believe we are heading toward chaos. God willing, let it not be violent."

< 8 >

Good Intentions

When I arrived in Cuba, the policy the United States was pursuing was that defined in the Cuban Democracy Act of 1992. The law, sponsored by Senator Robert Torricelli of New Jersey, was designed to strengthen the enforcement of the economic embargo and, at the same time, provide ways for the United States to reach out to the Cuban people. The second part, known as "Track Two," called for an increased flow of information to Cubans and for greater outreach to them through academic and cultural exchanges.

It was an excellent idea. The best way to change any closed society is to provide information. Ideally, the interaction between the citizens of the United States and those of Cuba would have encouraged understanding and ultimately brought about change. Fully implemented, Track Two would have provided intellectuals with one thing they crave: contact with the outside world. With almost all other nations, the United States promotes exchanges and provides information as part of normal cultural relations. The Cuban regime, however, saw the proposed expansion of the cultural relationship as a nefarious form of subversion. All things regarding the bilateral relationship are political, and the State viewed the Cuban Democracy Act as simply a morsel it did not want to swallow. Track Two was, in fact, sold in the United States as a way to undermine Castro. When it is promoted that way, why would Fidel see the expansion of the exchange of people and ideas as a positive step? The regime took umbrage with this policy, precisely because ideas bring change.

It is hard to implement a policy of any kind when the State goes on a rampage against it. The perceived threat of cultural exchanges and increased information inspired the Castro government to begin a strident campaign against Track Two. The Torricelli Act became the target of harangues published in *Granma*. Academics and intellectuals were sternly warned not to participate in exchanges. After all, such programs were, the State argued, designed not to expand intellectual contact but rather to subvert the Castro regime. Even Fidel spoke on the issue. On July 26, 1995, the anniversary of the attack on the Moncada barracks, he made this comment:

> The enemy does not falter in its determination to destroy us. There are two concepts: that of the extreme right in U.S. politics who dream of strangling us with an even stronger economic blockade, if this were possible, and erase us from the face of the earth by any means.
>
> The other concept is that of those who wish to infiltrate us, weaken us, to create all kinds of counterrevolutionary organizations, and destabilize the country regardless of the consequences. An entire theory has been designed, with a program designed for this purpose. These people want to extend their influence through broad exchanges with diverse sectors which they consider vulnerable, to grant doubtful scholarships and dazzle us with their billion dollar institutions, their technology, and their social research centers.
>
> They do not authorize Americans to travel to, tour, or vacation in Cuba, but they are willing to send our universities sociologists, philosophers, historians, Cuba experts, professors of English and other academics to impart knowledge among us. However, by no stretch of the imagination do they want to send a professor of cybernetics, computer technology, or any other technological area that has nothing to do with ideology and could be of some use to the country. In other words, these who pursue the so-called Track Two of the Torricelli Law are the ones who want to destroy us from within.

On August 17, 1995, Felix Pita Astudillo, an editorial writer who appears regularly in *Granma,* followed up Fidel's comments with a few embellishments. His talent seems to be finding creative ways of insulting the United States and maligning the Miami Cuban community. He saw Track Two as the U.S. placing scholarships, books, and intellectual opportunities as a tempting bait, a carrot, that would ultimately undermine the regime. One of his opinion pieces was titled: "The Poison Carrot: Do They Think Cubans Are Stupid?" He wrote:

> Fidel analyzed the two concepts which are prevalent in the breast of the Empire with relation to Cuba: those who dream of strangling us with an even stronger blockade which will wipe us from the face of the earth; and those who also want to exterminate us, but by penetration, by seeking for vulnerable areas, and by detecting and recruiting those who will take the offered carrot and those who put the egotistical ethic of having before the ethic of being and ultimately before the destabilization of the Revolution.
>
> The first, more obvious and known, want to fry the Revolution in boiling water. The second, more sneaky, prefer to roast us over the grill. But both have the same objective of restoring the old neocolonial plantation on the island. . . .
>
> The Revolution will not be destroyed from within nor from outside. It will not be destroyed by the stick, nor by carrots poisoned with counterrevolutionary venom.

As an American diplomat working for the goals of Track Two, I faced a daily trial because I was one of those "sneaky" ones who supposedly was trying to "roast [the Revolution] over the grill." No one wants to do harm, and yet I knew that any contact I had with Cubans could potentially harm them. Often I was walking on eggshells, being careful to not tread too often in one spot or ask too much of anyone. If someone established contact with me and then disappeared for weeks or months, I understood, because individuals had to think about self-preservation. The person appeared again when the political noose was not quite so tight. I knew that if I was not careful, the consequences could be grave. Indeed, contact with the U.S. Interests Section diplomats was the State's reason for throwing one well-respected professor, Gloria Leon, out of the Party and out of the University of Havana. The people who took the risk of being my friends in Havana were often questioned and occasionally harassed. Because of the regime's opposition to Track Two, by doing my job and sharing ideas and books that people were eager to read, I was, at times, putting people in political danger.

The State's opposition was a problem not just for those of us working on Track Two. American foundations and universities that had ongoing relationships with institutions on the island were caught in the crossfire. Because of Track Two, these organizations, which had nothing to do with U.S. government initiatives, became suspect. Where Cuban academics had once been friendly with visiting representives, they became cautious and uncomfortable. Because of the opposition of the State and the roadblocks placed in the way of exchanges and interaction, some foreign visitors considered Track Two to be dead by the end of 1995.

In spite of the State's condemnation of Track Two, some intellectuals were brave enough to not retreat and hide but rather to maintain their contacts with Americans. Jesús Vega, a man with piercing blue eyes and an intellect just as sharp, was one such person. The entry hall of the tiny apartment he shared with his wife and their two children was packed with books in several languages. Jesús could easily discuss, in English, Salman Rushdie's *The Satanic Verses,* which he had read in Italian. He was a known expert on Cuban film and well recognized in intellectual circles. When he was offered an opportunity to lecture at a prominent American university, it was at about the same time that *Granma* published one of its first articles about intellectuals who participated in exchanges with the United States. Jesús quickly came in to process his visa, fearing that the State might deny him the opportunity to travel. His boss, he said, nearly had an attack of nerves when Jesús came to him with the invitation letter. The man had exclaimed, "You are one of the Track Two people!" Jesús was granted his visa with little problem because he had traveled the year before and returned. He would have returned this time, but Raul Castro's speech at the Fifth Party Plenum made it clear that he would have problems if he did. Jesús, because of his creative independent thinking, had been called a counterrevolutionary as far back as his university days. There was no longer a place for him in Cuba. He applied for political asylum. His wife and children have since joined him in Florida.

Maritza, a University of Havana professor, is another person who stood her ground. She found herself on the wrong side of Track Two by committing the grave error of falling in love. An American professor who had paid numerous visits to the island had befriended Maritza and over the years had fallen in love with her. When they married, her colleagues began pointing fingers at her, accusing her of trying to leave the country and of being in bed with the CIA. She was considered the worst of the "trackers" even though her relationship had nothing to do with politics. I sat with her in her comfortable apartment as she lamented her situation. Because of the criticism and ultimately the shunning, she had left her position at the university. Her husband had returned to his teaching job in the United States, and she was left waiting, in a strange state of limbo, for her immigration petition to be approved. Although independent thinkers in Cuba have observed that they must choose to stay silent, go to prison, or leave the country, Maritza added another possible outcome from personal experience: to be ostracized within the system. She said the State is using this tactic more often now, because if it throws people out of work, it risks criticism from overseas. Instead, the State leaves people who do not completely toe the Party line in their positions, but they are not allowed to travel, and no one will socialize with them. They are within the system, not cast out as dissidents are, but they are not accepted as trusted members of the group, for they have declined to live by the *doble moral.*

The other element of Track Two was increasing the flow of information to Cuba. On the island, there is a hunger for information that cannot be assuaged. The books, pamphlets, and newspaper clippings that were given out by my office were devoured by readers and passed on to others. On a trip to the eastern part of Cuba, I dropped by a Casa de Cultura, a cultural center, in Guantanamo. I left a few pamphlets containing translations of works by American authors and a book of American poetry. The librarian of the cultural center was so moved that months later she called me during a visit to Havana to thank me and ask for more materials. I told her that I would be happy to give her more. She never appeared to collect the materials and never called back. I can only assume that she was warned not to contact me again.

Cuban think tanks and universities survive intellectually off the materials the U.S. Interests Section sends. Spanish translations of such books as Robert Reich's *The Work of Nations,* Lester Langley's *America and the Americas,* and Al Gore's *Earth in the Balance* are much in demand, as is Jorge Castañeda's *Utopia Unarmed.* Still, when word comes from on high in the Party that the ideologically pure Cuban will not read any materials like these, libraries will return boxes of books unopened, the University of Havana foreign languages department will return stacks of much needed American literature texts, and the international press center will return our newspaper clippings.

In general, I do not think the Cuban government had an objection to most of the books and pamphlets the Interests Section handed out. They did not like George Orwell's *Animal Farm,* but a University of Havana think tank did specifically request it. The State's objections mostly centered around books that dealt with the island. Whether the books came from us or other sources, any writings on Cuba that were not given the specific blessing of the regime were not supposed to be read. During her time in Cuba, the American diplomat who worked on human rights issues met almost daily with dissidents and often gave books to them. Most of the books were on general topics, but some were on human rights topics and others were about Cuba. When she departed the island, the number-two person on the Americas desk at the Cuban Ministry of Foreign Relations, Rafael Dausa, went on television and showed the "objectionable" books that she had been distributing. One book he held up contained the writings of José Martí, one of Cuba's greatest heroes and philosophers. The Revolution has carefully selected from Martí's works to support its own ends, but the book in question presented a broader collection of Martí's essays, some of which contradicted the Revolution.

Despite the resistance of the State and the many fits and starts of the bilateral relationship, cultural and academic contacts between the United States and Cuba are gradually increasing. Universities are expanding their programs, and musicians and artists are traveling back and forth across the straits of Florida. The thousands of books and other publications that have been given away in recent years have served as a reminder to intellectuals that ideas have a life of their own.

< 9 >

America!

For all of the State's efforts to cast the United States as the enemy, most Cubans hold a great affection for America. This affinity persists because many people either have personal experience in the United States or have relatives living there. Before the Revolution, there was a great deal of interaction between the two countries. Americans went to Cuba as tourists, and U.S. corporations carried on significant business on the island. Cuban families made vacation visits to the United States, and some students pursued their education there. Now, for those who are given permission to travel, the United States is the place to "go up for air" and take a break from the pain of life on the island. For the many people who have family and close friends in the United States, the personal ties help to perpetuate a positive image of "the enemy." Many families are separated by the Florida Straits, and though relatives may now be citizens of another country, they have not ceased to be family. It is difficult to condemn an entire nation when loved ones make up part of its citizenry.

Politics aside, Cuba and America share a great deal. Jazz, baseball, cars, movies, and even table manners hold common ground. Before 1959, jazz musicians from the two nations took inspiration from one another; Cuban and American jazz had a symbiotic relationship. In the years since the Revolution, jazz on the island, like so much else, has had to evolve along its own path. The tremendous talent and creativity of the musicians have been developing in a cocoon and are set to burst forth. Drummer Changuito was nominated for a Grammy. Pianist Chucho Valdes has played in Lincoln Center. Drummer Anga played with Roy Hargrove at the Village Vanguard in New York.

Closing night of the 1996 Cuban jazz festival was an unofficial celebration of the links between Cuban and American jazz. The stage was alive with the music of Chucho Valdes, Roy Hargrove, Ron Blake, Steve Coleman, and Cesar Lopez. I do not think a closer tie would have existed between these musicians if there were formal relations between the two countries, but then, as an American manager of a musician said, "Jazz is before borders." The elaborate dance of the music did not end when the curtain came down. The jam session continued at the Hotel Riviera until far beyond the wee hours of the morning. Cubans moved to the music. Americans danced expressively. Someone lit a joint. A singer from Los Angeles, Martica, with her hair in a crew cut, wove emotional lyrics into the saxophone sound of dreadlock-wearing Cuban Yosvany Terry. The stage got sexually charged when American Cecilia Noel took the microphone and bid seductive Cuban Cesar Lopez to come play his alto saxophone. The visiting Americans were surprised and impressed by the quality and creativity of the Cuban music. When the Americans pursued the relationship, inviting their new friends to the United States and also making return visits to the island, they were, in many ways, picking up on a beautiful friendship that had nearly been lost.

Baseball is another common passion of Cubans and Americans. In fact, the old General Motors slogan about things American, like hot dogs and apple pie, could be applied on the island with the slight variation to "Baseball, *congrí*, Coppelia, and Chevrolet."* The island has produced outstanding baseball players, a fact underlined when the national team took home the Olympic gold medal from Atlanta in 1996 and more recently when two Cuban pitchers played for World Series winners. Although U.S. major league games are not broadcast on Cuban radio, fans listen to the games on Miami and

---

* *Congrí* refers to the Cuban dish of black beans mixed with rice. Coppelia is the only brand of ice cream on the island.

Key West stations. Remarkably, there are rabid Atlanta Braves fans on the island. When I put a Braves pennant on my office door, two of them dropped by within fifteen minutes to take a look at it. They told me they stayed on top of how the team was doing throughout the season. Even Fidel admitted to supporting the Braves when they played in the World Series, but that may have had something to do with a friendship he has with the owner of the team. Why the mania for American baseball? Some can remember when a few American teams came to the island for spring training. Many have baseball card collections that date from before 1959.

The American love affair with the automobile is recognized around the world. But consider for a moment the Cubans' love for the cars from Detroit that they have been wed to for nearly forty years. The same American-made models have been on the road in Cuba since 1959, but they are still preferred to anything from Russia. Any male who likes cars can recognize the make and model of every Ford, Chevy, Chrysler, Oldsmobile, and Packard imported before the Revolution that still graces the roads. I fell into a pattern of talking about cars with two of these automobile aficionados whenever we drove anywhere together. They taught me that the slope of the trunk was the key to telling a 1940s car from a 1950s and that when looking at automobiles from the late fifties, the size of the fins characterize the model. They patiently told me the makes and models of the cars we saw, until I was recognizing them as well. Imagine my father's surprise when I came home for a visit and at an antique car show said, "That's a 1956 Chevy BelAir." These men do not just know what the models are. Many could take one of these cars apart and put it back together again. The necessity of keeping these American cars on the road has inspired an intimate knowledge of how they work.

When people began to earn a little money, the first thing many did was fix up their vintage cars. A hope held by some is that when change comes, they will be able to sell their cars to foreign collectors and make a tidy sum. For many, the vehicle is the only capital they have. Cubans thought my car, a 1994 two-door Ford Escort, was a sports car—after all, it was a two-door. When it arrived on the island, men at the office were very interested in it and could not stop talking about how attractive it was. From the first time I drove it, motorists who were stopped beside me at red lights would ask me if I wanted to trade cars. One wishful thinker offered me his bicycle. One day, I pulled up by a vintage car in very good condition with a Ford decal in the window. When I asked the man what year it was, his response was 1940. He said his car was the parent of mine.

It is not just American cars that Cubans love. People on the island have a preference for American brands in general. Despite the embargo, Coca-Cola is available everywhere, imported from Canada, Mexico, and Venezuela. Pepsi products are available as well, but not all Cubans are partial to Coke or Pepsi. For instance, when I offered a soft drink to one elderly man, he waxed nostalgic about Royal Crown Cola—his favorite drink before the Revolution. American brand names have become part of the local idiom. What is Scotch tape called in Havana? Scotch tape. A vacuum cleaner? Not an *aspiradora*, but a Hoover. That refrigerator in the corner? It is a Frigidaire—even if it is Soviet made. One man told me proudly that he had just managed to buy an [old] washing machine. He said, "It's American. A Whirlpool!" A few words like "elevator" have been lifted from the English language. When I asked why Cubans did not use "*ascensor*" instead of "*elevador*," someone quipped, "An '*ascensor*' goes up and down. An '*elevador*' goes up and down but never works." Actually, I rode in quite a few Otis elevators that are still functioning after nearly forty years of little maintenance.

American movies are a mainstay of entertainment on the island. Subtitled films are shown on television on two weekday evenings and a double feature of recent American releases is shown on Saturday night. In the movies, Cubans find a bit of escape and also catch a glimpse of the forbidden nation to the north. Old-timers told me that before the Revolution, Hollywood film companies would sometimes screen movies on the island before releasing them in the United States, saying that they wanted to test the movies on a good trial audience before giving them general release. Although those days are long gone, the passion for American cinema has not paled, even through the years that Soviet influence was prevalent. As one gray-haired man with blue eyes griped about actions of the State over the years, he acknowledged, "At least he [Fidel] never cut us off from American movies." When television airs a European or Latin American movie, some people watch. When the movie is American, everyone stays home. On Saturday nights, families often will spend the evening out in the fresh air on the Malecón. Just before ten o'clock, though, they start drifting home to catch the beginning of the double feature. Abel Prieto, the long-haired fortysomething head of UNEAC, the Cuban Union of Writers and Artists, explained that although the regime preferred not to show American films because of the images and messages that do not support the ideals of the Revolution, it continued to show them because doing so is economical; the State does not pay for the rights. The regime is rather cagey about the source of the films, but it must be a good source: *Braveheart* hit the Saturday movies well before it was shown on Home Box Office in the United States. One professor said, "I would be happy if there were nothing on television except movies and the news." The Cubans loved *The Lion King, Fried Green Tomatoes,* and *Forrest Gump.*

At a formal dinner one evening with guests from both nations, I noticed that we were all using similar table manners. Most Latin Americans eat like Europeans, keeping both hands on the table. In this group—whether it was representative I do not know—the Cubans, like the Americans, had one hand in their laps and one on the table.

A myriad of little ties link the two nations together. America is the place of dreams and home to family. Despite the shared interests, however, it is also what the State terms the "enemy" of Cuba. Holding a potentially enormous influence over the island's future, America, the promised land, is also the "evil empire" to the north. It is at once salvation and damnation.

< 10 >

Migration

I was sitting on a beach east of Havana with American friends gazing out at the horizon where the azure sea met the sky when one of them commented, "And ninety miles out there is freedom." It is precisely the promise of political and economic freedom that motivated tens of thousands of Cubans to take to rafts in August 1994. That was not the first time. Cubans have been seeking refuge in the United States for generations. José Martí spent half of his life in America. Even Fidel spent time in what Martí called "the belly of the beast." The United States, or "La Yuma" as it is sometimes called, is the promised land. It is the way out. It is the way to the future. In Poland in 1986, a student said to me, "Every citizen of an oppressed country has two homelands, his own and the United States." For Cubans this statement is even more true because of the geographical proximity and the historical ties. Taking to the sea in a raft is a risky venture, yet the young have been driven to it by their lack of hope for the future, and others have seen it as the only way to escape the political and economic difficulties that make life nearly impossible.

When I arrived in Havana in February 1995, I saw the aftermath and the pain of the August exodus. One catalyst that precipitated the flood of rafters was the rapid spread of stories about the sinking of the *13 de Marzo*. The one-hundred-year-old tugboat had chugged out of the harbor to the open sea in the predawn hours of July 14, loaded with men, women, and children fleeing the island. According to survivors, the boat was followed by several other tugboats that, once the *13 de Marzo* was several miles from shore, used water cannons to spray the decks and then proceeded to ram the tug. Forty-one people on board died. A few weeks later, on August 4, disturbances erupted on the Malecón. The unrest was quelled by Fidel's arrival on the scene. Sweltering summer heat and shortages of electricity and goods were turning Havana into a pressure cooker.

In response to the situation, the State quietly opened an escape valve. Although attempting to leave the island, *salida ilegal* (illegal exit or departure), remained a crime punishable by imprisonment, word traveled quickly that the authorities were looking the other way. Hastily assembled rafts consisting of inner tubes, wood, bamboo, and other materials that would float were lashed together and carried down the streets to the sea. The mood was enthusiastic and hopeful. All that the aspiring emigrants had to do was make it into international waters, twelve miles offshore, and they were bound for the promised land.

Approximately 30,000 of these *balseros* (rafters) were rescued in international waters and made it to the United States. A great many, however, met a different fate. Rafts sank or were hit by waves large enough to wash people overboard. Some *balseros* drank seawater and died of dehydration. Just how many perished in the attempt to leave the island is not known, but estimates range easily into the thousands. When political activist and dissident Francisco Chaviano tried to compile a list of the names of those lost, he found himself imprisoned. Family members who stayed behind hoped and prayed for news that loved ones had successfully made the crossing. Often that news did not come. Individuals seemed to simply have disappeared, and there was no real way to mourn. There was no funeral mass. The nation had to swallow its tears. People grieved silently for the sons, daughters, and friends who had been consumed by an unfriendly sea.

One retired professional man, a former revolutionary, told me in an emotional voice:

> I fought in the streets against Batista. We all sacrificed a lot. Sure, we had a good time. Those were heady days. We were building a new future. We were building a new world for our children. Now my children are grown and what do they have? They have no

hope. No future. My son was a high school science teacher—and a good one. He just quit his job. He has a family and cannot support them on 300 pesos a month. He is looking for a job in the dollar sector. My other son is a *balsero*. He left last summer. He was seventeen when he left. We tried to discourage him from leaving. We talked many times. He knew we did not want him to take the risk. One morning in August [1994] we woke to find him not in the house. He left a note for us on the car. He is a good boy, you know. All the teenagers in the neighborhood rafted. I do not know how many made it. We live so close to the sea. He loves the sea. He used to go diving for shells. We had no word from him for three weeks. He was in Panama and then Guantanamo. We learned he was safe through Radio Martí. He is in Miami now. My cousins are taking care of him. I have not seen them in thirty-five years, but they are good people. He is in school, learning English, and working very hard. Here he did not study. He had no reason to study. Here he had no future. Now he is studying and working. He will do just fine. He is a good boy, you know.

The tragic outcome for so many of the August 1994 rafters did not stem the rising desire of Cubans, particularly the young, to leave the island. I had been in Cuba a few months when I heard the song "Hotel California" on a local radio station. The song caught my attention because it was so relevant to the island. Cubans with a knowledge of English must have related to it as well, because before long, the song was played all over the island, on the radio and in discotheques; there was even a salsa version. In early February 1996, I met Peter, a bartender at his cousin's *paladar* and a trained English teacher. While the radio played "Hotel California," I listened to this young man, who has mentally checked out of the country but has not been able to leave. "I speak English and I am learning Italian," he said. "There is a cruise ship that arrives every week, and I hope I can get a job with the cruise line. There is no future here. I do not know if things will ever change. Foreigners tell me things will change, and that there is a future; I do not know. It is hard to believe there is." Young Cubans have studied hard and earned degrees only to find they cannot make a living. The only way out that most of them see is leaving the country. Gustavo Arcos, a leading dissident, said, "For most of the young people, being Cuban is just an unfortunate accident of birth."

Parents are aware of the dreams of their children and will do whatever they can to improve their lives. An artist who was only ten years old when the Revolution took place told me, "My daughter wants to leave Cuba. I do not want to leave because this is my country. She is talking about going to Venezuela with her boyfriend, but I do not want her to go there because she would basically be alone. If she were in America, my family could look after her. Maybe I could arrange for my cousin to marry her—the two surnames are different." He did not have to pursue the sham marriage. His daughter and her boyfriend are now married and living in Florida with their infant child. One mother of a twenty-five-year-old professional said, "My son is desperate to leave. So many want to leave, to escape. Sometimes I think if you could just scoop up the entire population of Cuba and drop it in the United States, we would all be a lot happier."

Leaving the island is a big step. In many ways, those who leave are seen as abandoning the Revolution and are branded as traitors. A tall man with green eyes told me:

> I am having trouble at work. They are questioning my loyalty to the Revolution. My son's mother left for the United States as a political refugee. She asked for him to join her in America. He wanted to go to her. I signed the release form, since a minor cannot leave without parental consent. They said I should not have let him go. He is sixteen and old enough to make the choice. She is alone there. I have my wife and my mother. His mother needs

him. I think it will be better for him because he will have a better future there. My boss called me in and gave me the official scolding for letting my son abandon Cuba and the Revolution. Then she said, "As a mother, I do not blame you. If I were alone in a new country and my son's father let my boy come to me, I would think he had done the right thing."

For those on the island already branded as traitors because of their dissident views, legal migration is a solution. Former political prisoners, disestablished professionals, and those persecuted for their religious or political beliefs have the option of applying for refugee status at the U.S. Interests Section. A bearded poet whose writing had irritated the regime said to me in an anguished tone, "I must leave. The authorities will not let me move or write. What do I have here? I cannot work. My daughters are young now, only eight and ten, but in a few years, what will keep them from taking to the streets as *jineteras*? They will see that as the best way to make dollars and improve our lives. I must leave here so that will not happen."

An outspoken red-headed independent journalist who came to my office stridently recounted her history as a dissident and her time in prison and then asked if I could check on her application for refugee status. "I want to keep going in my work," she said, "Someone has to fight. But the last time I was detained, they threatened to take my children away from me. My little girls are my life. I am so afraid they will take them from me." Her story points out what is happening increasingly to opposition figures and independent thinkers. The State is threatening them with prison if they do not leave, effectively forcing into exile those individuals they do not want on the island. Independent journalist Rafael Solano, after being held for six weeks in solitary confinement, was given a choice: leave the island as quickly as possible or be tried on charges of enemy propaganda and illegal association and go to jail for over ten years. Solano left the island for Spain.

Leaving is, for many, the ultimate way to *resolver* the problems of life in Cuba. People who have no means of leaving fantasize about ways out. When I mentioned at a party that I was taking my young dog and cat, animals that had been abandoned on the streets of Havana, to the United States as "adopted children," an engineer commented, "Oh, if only we could all just turn ourselves into cats and dogs." Another man asked me how big the cage was for the dog, wondering if he might fit inside.

While many do see leaving as a panacea, there are others who have made a conscious decision to stay. Their resolve derives from a mixture of defiance and hope. One professor who decided long ago to remain on the island said to me, "As long as I am here, this country cannot belong to them [the State]. This is my country. As long as I am here, they cannot have it all because they do not have me." The commitment and patriotism of a young mulatto father were evident when he explained, "I had a chance to leave. My parents and my brothers are all in the United States. I am staying. Someone has to change this place."

< II >

The Migration Accords

You do not need to issue 20,000 visas, you just need to
issue two . . . to Fidel and Raul.
—a joke

One evening, my neighbor came to me asking for help for two young men who wanted to emigrate. I was tired after a long day and told her frankly, "This country belongs to the Cuban people. If you all would put as much time and energy into making it what you want as you put into trying to leave it, you might have a different country." She looked a bit shamefaced and said, "I guess we are looking for the easy way out." That "easy way out" was cut off on May 2, 1995, when U.S. Attorney General Janet Reno announced that all future rafters picked up on the high seas would be returned to Cuba.

Eight months earlier, on September 9, 1994, in an effort to end the rafting crisis, Cuba and the United States had reached an agreement on migration. That accord guaranteed the legal immigration to the United States of at least 20,000 people every year. In return, the Cubans agreed to stop the hemorrhage of humanity that had been spilling unchecked from the island. There was no ending date on the agreement. The United States usually grants no more than 20,000 immigrant visas per year to citizens of most countries; under this accord, however, the United States agreed to grant no *fewer* than 20,000 to Cuban citizens.

After the September accord was signed, rescued rafters were taken to Guantanamo Naval Base on the eastern tip of the island. From Guantanamo, many of them were gradually paroled into the United States for medical or humanitarian reasons. A point was reached in the spring of 1995 when all of the women, children, and elderly had been sent to the United States, leaving about 20,000 young, able-bodied men in the camps in Guantanamo. Tensions were rising, and there were concerns about violence, not just between the Cubans but between the Cubans and the American soldiers. In addition, there was a question as to what would happen when summer, the rafting season because the seas are calm, arrived and more people took to the seas.

The announcement of the May 2 accord reverberated through the island. A door had slammed closed. With the word that rafters would be returned to the island, the escape route was cut off. While Cubans recognized the loss of one route off the island, they also realized that the action would save lives. Some with more dissident leanings saw the door closing as a way to turn up the heat on the regime. If unhappy Cubans could not just jump on a raft, they might have to stay on the island and might put the energies of their frustration behind bringing change to the island. The goal of both countries in signing the accords was and is safe, orderly, and legal migration. The governments wanted to prevent the loss of life at sea. The Cuban government felt it had gained a great deal through the accords. The fact that rafters had always been welcomed with open arms in America was a thorn in its side. With the change, *balseros* were being treated much like rafters from any other Caribbean country. As far as the Cuban government and many citizens were concerned, the nation's sovereignty was being recognized. For the United States, the May 2 accord provided a way to encourage legal migration, not rafting. It is unlikely that any U.S. president would like to see thousands upon thousands of rafters hit the shores of Florida as they did in 1994. As long as those picked up at sea were being taken to the United States, there was an incentive for people to raft. The accord also solved the problem of tension at Guantanamo. As part of the agreement, the United States would accept all those in Guantanamo who were not specifically excluded by migration laws. The "excludables" included people who had committed violent crimes or had previously been deported from the United States. Not counting them, there were about 15,000 men in Guantanamo whom the United States agreed to accept, freeing them from the no-man's-land of life in a camp. Over the next three years, their numbers were credited toward the 20,000 visas to be issued by the U.S. Interests Section.

Only three days after the May 2 accord was announced, the first return of Cuban rafters occurred. Because there would be media coverage and I was the press spokesman for the Interests Section, I was tapped to go to the site. Consular officers Sandra Salmon and Ted O'Connor, Coast Guard Commander J. D. Dale, Immigration and Naturalization Service officer Alfonso Piñeda, and I set out for an hour-long drive to the town of Cabañas. There we were met by Cuban officials from the Foreign Ministry and the Interior Ministry. Together, we rode across the bay in a high-powered speedboat that had been confiscated from narcotics traffickers. Taking the overland route to the pier would have meant an additional hour of driving. As we sped across the water, I marveled at the beauty of the unspoiled coastline, where mangroves clung to the water's edge. I looked up at the remarkably clear blue sky and appreciated the feel of the sun and wind on my face. Still, my nerves were taut, because I knew that I was in the middle of an extraordinary event.

Members of the Coast Guard lined the deck of the 210–foot cutter *Durable,* which was transporting the rafters, as we approached it and slowed. We then made our way to the pier Añescos, an abandoned concrete shipping pier for sugar that extends out from a lush green coastline. Except for a dirt road leading to the pier, there were no signs of development. When we pulled in, the press, which was making the trip by bus, had not yet arrived. We waited for the cutter and the press with an unspoken anxiety. No one knew how events were going to unfold. What if the rafters did not want to get off the cutter? We were haunted by the memory of repatriations in Asian countries that had ended with people being forcibly carried off airplanes. What if, as Ted O'Connor imagined, the rafters linked arms and started singing "We Shall Overcome"?

As the cutter docked, young members of the Cuban Coast Guard, dressed in t-shirts, shorts, and plastic shoes, caught the ropes thrown down and secured them. Then, for the first time since the Revolution, the American flag was raised on an official U.S. vessel in Cuban waters. No Cubans were to board the cutter, and no Americans were to disembark. Our delegation boarded. Sandra Salmon and Ted O'Connor spoke to the rafters and informed them of the various options for legal migration. The rafters were reluctant to leave, but Ted was persuasive in letting the rafters know that the cutter was not a cruise ship. Once the first person left, the others proceeded to disembark. The group had been plucked from the sea by a Caribbean cruise ship before being passed to the Coast Guard, so they were dressed in white shorts printed with blue anchors and bright yellow t-shirts that announced "I'm Ship Shape." They walked 100 yards down the pier accompanied by State social workers and boarded a bus.

When they were all on the bus, I walked the same path down the pier to land, where about fifty members of the press were waiting and ready to pounce. They surrounded me, pushing and shoving. I had always wondered what it was like when microphones and cameras were put in your face with no sense of control. Surprisingly, as I heard many questions, I filtered them out and found one that I actually could answer. I walked away from the crush laughing—it had been an incredible rush. As I walked back out the pier, the cutter was moving away from the dock. All of us were feeling euphoric—the first official U.S.-Cuban collaboration had worked. We boarded the fast boat and headed back. About halfway to Cabañas, the captain throttled back, and the Cubans offered us beer, crackers, cheese, and fresh pineapple. We toasted the success. It was an historic moment, and we were all caught up in the tremendous release that came after the tension. I made the trip to meet returned rafters six more times. We all began to relax a bit, and on one occasion as we waited for the cutter to arrive, one Cuban actually took out his fishing pole and started casting.

The Lottery

Before the September accord was signed, the United States issued only a few thousand immigrant visas or paroles (provisional status immigrant visas) to Cubans each year. These visas were all issued either to relatives of American citizens or to refugees, especially dissidents and former political prisoners. Issuing 20,000 immigration documents instead of that few thousand required a tremendous effort and a great deal of creative planning. The most important initiative was the implementation of the Special Cuban Migration Program, or lottery. Winners received the chance to have an immigrant visa interview, something that would otherwise have been reserved only for those whose immediate relatives were American citizens. To enter the lottery, a person had to be over the age of eighteen and meet one of several basic requirements that included having completed high school or having held a job for a few years. Most Cubans met the qualifications and so could enter the lottery by simply addressing an envelope to the U.S. Interests Section and putting their name, address, and identification number in the return address corner.

The first lottery, held in November and December 1994, netted over 189,000 entries. The winners had to show that they had complied with the rules of the lottery and that they qualified under the laws of immigration of the United States before the visas were issued. In the first year of the accord, about one-third of the 20,000 immigrants were lottery winners. Doctors, journalists, college students, and people from many other walks of life traveled to the United States as a result of the program. Even though the notification envelopes were sent through the local mail, the drivers distributing USIS materials would be approached as they made deliveries and asked, "Is that for me? Is that from the lottery?"

When the second round of the lottery opened on March 15, 1996, the Interests Section expected a good response. What happened was extraordinary. By the time the last entries were received—they had to be postmarked by April 30—the mission had received over 436,000 envelopes. The enormous response carried a powerful message: More than 436,000 Cubans between eighteen and fifty-five, despite the possible consequences of their actions, were actively seeking to change their lives. As far as the Cuban government was concerned, the first day that people could enter the lottery produced a riot. People entering the lottery desperately wanted to bypass the Cuban mail system either because they were afraid their entries would not be delivered or because they were concerned that the State would take retribution against them for submitting an entry. Many wanted to deliver their envelopes directly to the U.S. Interests Section. Crowds gathered on the roads and in the parks near the Section, but Cuban security kept them at bay. Several times, Americans went out to the park and collected hundreds of entries in plastic grocery bags. As one man deposited his entry, he cried jubilantly, "Goal!!!"—the well-known soccer cry. When a van with diplomatic license plates drove by the crowd on its way to the Section, the driver was surprised by several thousand envelopes being shoved through an open window. Eventually the Cuban government set up drop boxes and the crowds dissipated. On that first day, we received 14,307 entries. By the third day, we had over 30,000. The drop boxes at the Section, which visitors and employees stuffed every day, were large cardboard boxes appropriately wrapped in red gift paper. I personally received quite a few entries. My neighbors approached me on the street as I walked my dog and surreptitiously slipped me entries. My doorbell was rung late one evening by someone who had an envelope for me. My horseback-riding instructor quietly handed me a stack one day after a lesson. The lottery meant hope for people looking for a way out. For those who entered, there was the feeling that they had found the light at the end of the tunnel.

Upholding the Accord

As mentioned earlier, both the United States and Cuba benefit from the migration accords. The United States does not want to see thousands of Cubans washing up on Florida's shores, and Cuba does not want the world to see people fleeing the island. But more important, neither government wants people swimming with sharks and dying in the Florida Straits when there are safe and legal ways to get from one country to the other.

In the wake of the agreement on migration, there were abundant, but ultimately unfounded, rumors that better relations between the two nations were just around the corner. However, the reality is that balancing Washington, Havana, and Miami politics can be tricky, especially when certain elements on both sides would like to see the accords fail. The U.S.-Cuba relationship is tenuous, and it seemed in the early months that almost every bilateral issue could undermine the agreement. Returning rafters, for example, became a sticky proposition on both sides. For the Cuban government, the sore point was that rafters who were determined by U.S. officials to have a credible fear of persecution were not returned. This meant that, occasionally, two or three rafters of a group would be taken to the United States. The Castro regime preferred that everyone be returned. On the U.S. side, the challenge came from those who claimed the Castro regime was persecuting the rafters who were returned. While most of the returnees had no difficulties and went back to their jobs, there were a few who had problems. Some had escaped from prison before taking to rafts and were sent back to prison to finish their terms. One returnee refused to take a job at the same salary level at the university where he had worked because it was not the same job—it was research instead of teaching. These cases received attention in the U.S. press, and, given the opposition of many Miami

Cubans to the accords, often seemed to have the potential to bring down the agreement. In fact, some returned rafters decided to just bide their time because they were convinced the accords would not last for long and they would soon be able to raft again and this time reach the United States.

As part of the May 2 accord, the U.S. Interests Section was to monitor the situation of the returned rafters to check that they were not facing harassment or discrimination. I had the opportunity to go to the eastern end of the island on one of these monitoring trips, where I visited the homes of rafters in Santiago de Cuba, Guantanamo, Banes, and Mayari. My colleague Cob Blaha and I arrived in Santiago de Cuba with names and addresses of individuals, rented a Jeep-like vehicle, and went looking. After consulting a map, we found the street where one of them lived. After driving around the block a few times, an action that became a common occurrence as we tried to find obscure addresses, we made it to the door of the man's home. We were told he was not there. Fortunately, someone knew where he was—he had moved back in with his ex-wife, just down the block. When we tracked him down, he became our guide, helping us find several of the others in the city.

At our second stop, a gray-haired woman wearing an ill-fitting cotton dress met us at the door of her humble home. On the street she explained that her son was not home but that he might be with his father. As tears rolled down her cheeks, she told us, with words from her evangelical faith, of the heartache her son had caused her in his young life. From her account, he had quite a list of petty criminal offenses to his credit. When we found his father's home on the outskirts of the city, we made our way past a gate and into a small overgrown yard strewn with odd bits and pieces of metal. Kittens played at my feet as we spoke with a balding man with a grizzled beard. He claimed that he had not seen his son in days and imagined that he had left again on a raft. Just as we had given up hope, the young man rode up on a bicycle.

We asked the rafters whether they knew about the accords and why they took to the sea. All of them knew about the agreement—they just thought they might get lucky. Cob and I also asked whether they had jobs and how the authorities were treating them. Most had been unemployed before they rafted and were still in that condition. One was trying to get a license to be a street vendor. None reported any political problems. Most of their living situations were comparable to those of average Cubans. The majority of their homes had a television, but there were few niceties. Luis, a very charming black man, lived with his wife and beautiful five-year-old daughter in an old wooden building with high ceilings. His motorcycle, an obvious luxury, was parked out front. We sat in wooden rocking chairs as we talked about his experience. His wife offered us coffee and his daughter smiled shyly at us as she played. From his home, we went to the apartment of Alejandro, a friend of the rafter with the petty crime record. When we arrived, he was not home, but as we were chatting with his mother, he walked up the stairs and into the apartment. He was wearing sunglasses, brightly colored shorts, and a baseball cap; he looked very much like a California surfer dude. He was also wearing white tennis shoes, just like the ones Luis had worn. I realized that these mementos of their adventure were being shown off like status symbols. Alejandro's family was of a different social level than the others we visited. The furniture and decorative items in their home were of finer quality. Alejandro's sister danced in a ballet company, and his father was eloquent and up-to-date on world events.

After we had checked on all the returnees in Santiago, we traveled to the other cities. In Mayari, we went to the home of a rafter who had been returned just a few days before. We drove to an address on the outskirts of town, where a woman answered the door and invited us in. An aging plastic flower arrangement sat on the Soviet-made television set. The woman told us that her son had already left again, this time for the Bahamas, hoping to eventually make it to the United States. Apparently he had been successful, for she said he had called his girlfriend from the Bahamas when he arrived. On the road into the town of Mayari there is a sign that reads "Here we are all happy." Right. The one who was not has already left.

When events occur that threaten the accords, they must be handled carefully because Castro holds and will continue to hold the "migration card." If Fidel chooses, he can open the gates again, and the straits will be flooded with Cubans. One such potentially explosive event occurred on Sunday, July 7, 1996, when Lieutenant Colonel Jose Fernandez Pupo hijacked a plane en route from Santiago to Guantanamo and forced it to land at Guantanamo Naval Base. National Assembly President Ricardo Alarcon said he expected the hijacker to be returned to the island in accordance with the Migration Accords or for him to be prosecuted. Subsequently, Miguel Alfonso, the Foreign Ministry spokesman, made it clear that if Pupo were not returned, the State would consider it a violation of the accords. The Cuban government's implied warning was that if Pupo were not returned to Cuba, where he was likely to face a firing squad, a wave of rafters could be unleashed. The United States is supposed to admit people as asylum seekers if they have a credible fear of persecution, and there is little doubt that a firing squad is persecution. Yet, if it admitted Pupo, it risked having thousands of Cubans take to the seas. Five different groups of rafters were, in fact, picked up over that weekend. The situation was apparently defused when Pupo was indicted for hijacking in the United States on October 23, 1996.

Given all the ins and outs of U.S-Cuba relations, both sides are doing a good job of fulfilling the accords. The agreements are not perfect, but they have, so far, sharply reduced the number of Cubans who risk their lives on the open sea.

Saying Farewell

Watching the faces of those who obtain immigration papers from the Americans and then the *tarjeta blanca*, or permission to leave

Cuba, is like watching a metamorphosis. The drawn faces are suddenly animated, and eyes begin to sparkle with a new light. Every departure is bittersweet, though, because those emigrating leave behind family and friends. They never know when they will see one another again. The airport is a tremendously emotional place because so many of the departures are permanent. Family and friends gather at the chain-link fence near the tarmac to wave and to cry. It is not easy to decide to leave the island. It is home, and it is Cuba.

< 12 >

News and Information

We maintain and will continue to maintain that the genuinely
free press is that which serves the freedom of the people.
—Raul Castro

The State completely controls the press in Cuba, including radio,
television, and print media. Watching the national evening news on
television can provide an education on what the government is focusing on, but the coverage does not reflect much about what is really going on in the country. The evening news always carries a lead
story on the successful sugar harvest or the tremendous potato harvest. That story is followed by one about yet another advance in the
tourism sector. Throw in a report on a very important visit by a foreign dignitary—or, better yet, a group of young socialists—and the
evening domestic news is covered. The international news is about
riots, strikes, terrorism, war, crime, and corruption. Of course, there
has to be at least one very negative report on the United States. One
professional woman commented, tongue in cheek, "After I watch
the news, I thank God I live in Cuba. The rest of the world is in ter-
rible shape." I knew that I had been watching the news and reading
Granma too much when I started wondering whether the United
States really was a nice place to live.

International radio stations broadcasting from Spain, the Netherlands, and the United States offer relief from the State monopoly.
Of the various international stations, U.S. government sponsored
Radio Martí probably has the most listeners. The Cuban government is no friend to the station, and its broadcasts, considered a propagandistic tool of the evil imperialists to the north, are relatively

effectively jammed by the State. There are, however, times and frequencies at which the signal is clear and people do tune in. Because they have to be circumspect about listening to Radio Martí, they refer to it as "Radio Pepe" and "Radio Casualidad." *Pepe* is the diminutive of the Cuban patriot Martí's first name, *José*. *Por casualidad* means "by chance," as in "I was tuning my radio and '*por casualidad*' I came across this station." Hence, Radio Casualidad.

From years of living with a censored State-controlled press, people have learned to read between the lines to figure out what is happening. They take the information from State news sources, international radio station reports, and personal experiences and mesh it all together to arrive at the closest they can come to a perception of reality. They are careful not to trust any one source. It is easy to see how this mixture of sources can create some fantastic rumors. One rumor circulating around Cuba was that all of the people on the island who had applied for the worldwide visa lottery program, who numbered in the thousands, were going to be awarded visas to the United States. In reality, a total of fewer than two hundred people were going to be selected. Without a free press, such rumors run rampant and are at least as credible as information from the State-run press.

Despite the need to keep pumping out propaganda, the press has not escaped the austerity of recent years. Of the three daily papers published before the Special Period, two are now weeklies and the other, *Granma*, though still produced daily, is published in a much reduced format. *Granma* covers the news, political commentary, sports, and the arts in its eight pages, which are the same size as the paper used in U.S. tabloids. The publishers are dealing with scarcity of paper, poor quality printing ink, and worn-out Soviet presses that have no replacement parts. It is a wonder that anything is published. The newsrooms do not resemble even small university newspaper offices. There are few if any computers. There is no sense of urgency. Journalists repeatedly write stories that will never see newsprint.

They censor themselves because they know of the constraints within which they write. *Granma,* by the way, is the name of the wooden yacht on which Fidel and his compatriots sailed to Cuba from Mexico in 1956 when they were beginning the Revolution. Rumor has it that the previous owner, an American, had named the craft for a cherished relative: his grandmother.

Independent Journalists

The State dominates the airwaves and the written press, but there are voices on the periphery that are making themselves heard despite the State monopoly. These voices of independent journalists are heard on the island because Radio Martí broadcasts their stories. Many of the independents were previously employed as journalists for the State. At some point, each of them came to a parting of the ways with the regime. Whether they were thrown out of their jobs or quit, they faced a difficult decision: Do I stay silent, or do I take the risk of imprisonment and go to work as an independent to try to tell the real story of what is happening on this island?

Those who take the risk are demonstrating courage. They are going up against tremendous odds, and if they lose, they can be charged with, among other things, enemy propaganda. These people are harassed. Their apartments are searched; their typewriters and computers—if they have them—are confiscated; they are detained; their homes are watched by the police; and yes, they are imprisoned. Most independent journalists type their stories on manual typewriters using whatever paper they can find. While they could benefit from training in modern journalistic techniques and while their style does run to the literary, they are at this point among the only voices in the information void on the island. They send their written stories to the *Miami Herald* and *El Nuevo Herald,* and they place verbal reports with Radio Martí. Their stories are now also carried on the Internet, a practice that started when journalists for CubaPress, an independent agency, began reading their stories over the telephone to colleagues in the United States who posted the information on an Internet web site. The State likes to claim there is freedom of the press in Cuba because independent journalists are allowed to send their stories to Radio Martí and have them broadcast back to the island.

Because of the difficulties they face, independent journalists can rarely stay active for long. Most of those I knew were forced to leave the island, but others have now filled their shoes. One of the first Cubans I met was a distinguished, if fragile, elderly gentleman by the name of Nestor Baguer who is an independent journalist. Nestor has lived and worked abroad, has an excellent command of English, and has strong opinions on how journalism should be done. Nestor was the backbone of the Cuban Association of Independent Journalists (APIC) while Yndamiro Restano, the association's leader and cofounder, was in prison for political reasons. APIC placed stories in the *Miami Herald* and was, for a time, the best known of the independent press agencies. Often, when journalists left the State and chose to work as independents, they went first to work for APIC.

Nestor is quite a character, walking the streets of Havana in a trademark black beret. He has a fondness for the ladies and was known not only to flirt outrageously but also to propose marriage on occasion to women decades his junior. Nestor does not get around well these days. His frail bones are not permitting him to do what he would like. The Cuban government is not terribly fond of him. Since, on the island, people over seventy cannot be sent to prison, the worst he told me that could happen to him was house arrest. In 1995 he was knocked down on the street on two occasions. On one of them the perpetrators yelled, "Counterrevolutionary!" Nestor has been in close contact with Reporters Without Borders. The group supplied him with a fax machine, which was later confiscated by the State. It also presented him with an Apple notebook computer, which was his pride and joy. He took great care to hide these tools of the trade with neighbors and friends because he knew that State Security could search his apartment and take his possessions at any time.

I met Rafael Solano not long after I arrived in Cuba. This young, intelligent, energetic man had been a star journalist at Radio Rebelde and had, several years earlier, won the coveted Premio Rey de España (King of Spain's Prize). He proudly showed me photos that had been taken of him with King Juan Carlos of Spain when he was awarded the international journalism prize. Unfortunately, his prizes did not make him immune from political problems at the radio station. These problems culminated in his leaving his position and joining forces with the independents shortly after I arrived in Cuba. After working with APIC for a while, he broke off and formed his own organization, Habana Press, which was to be dedicated to investigative reporting. He was excited and hopeful about doing independent journalism and working without the constraints of State censorship. Soon his stories were on Radio Martí and his name was appearing in the *Miami Herald*. He was aware of the risk he was running. He spoke to me once of his concern that he could be arrested and disappear.

Over the time I knew him, I could tell how things were going by his physical appearance. When things were difficult, he became gaunt; when he was receiving money and eating, he would get plump. He was, for me, a symbol of the hope for independent journalism. He was a new face with a strong mind and personality dedicated to the cause. If he could succeed, it seemed the movement might grow. The period from spring 1995 to February 1996 was a heady time for the independent journalists, whose ranks were growing and whose efforts were attracting international attention and financial support. In February 1996, during the crackdown on the human rights organization Concilio Cubano, I held my breath for a number of friends. Solano was among them. While many figures from the opposition and from independent journalism were detained and then released, some were held and not released. Solano was one of that small group.

He spent six weeks in solitary confinement with the light left burning twenty-four hours a day. He came to see me when he was released. I remember his statement, "They did not beat me." There are, however, other kinds of torture. He insisted that he would keep working, but the State was threatening him with over ten years in jail for enemy propaganda and illegal association. His colleagues encouraged him to leave. His confinement had affected all of them. As one said to me, "He says he is okay, but he is not. They really messed him up." Solano left for Spain very shortly after his release from confinement.

His compatriot at Habana Press, Julio Martinez, who once worked as a journalist for the labor union newspaper *Trabajadores,* was, perhaps, in the worst shape politically and physically of anyone I knew. Solano was the star who made headlines. Julio Martinez, who was charged with the same crimes, was forgotten. Because of illness and fear of detention, he went into hiding at a Catholic institution for the infirm around the time Solano was detained. When his health improved somewhat, he came to see me. He appeared disheveled and fearful. He explained that he did not know what to do. He was going to have to leave his refuge because his health was improving, but he had no place to go. His only relative, a sister, could not take him in, and the Cuban government had made clear its intention to charge him with the crimes of enemy propaganda and illegal association. I do not know if he found a solution.

When I first met Olance Nogueras, I thought that if there were a future for independent journalism, I was looking at it. In his late twenties, tall, intelligent, handsome, and motivated, this independent soul did investigative reporting on, among other topics, the Juragua nuclear plant. I knew he was willing to take big risks when he told me he had attended a press briefing at the State's Center for International Press. Some weeks later he attended another one, and this time he stood, introduced himself as an independent journalist, and asked a question. The Foreign Ministry Spokesman Miguel Alfonso actually answered the question. Olance, however, was ordered to leave and never come back. Before becoming an independent, Olance had worked at a provincial radio station. There, he started taking risks with what he put on the air during his time slot. The event, he told me, that cost him his job was an interview with a priest. During my last months in Cuba, I knew Olance was considering leaving the island because of the harassment he and his family were facing. He came to the United States in August 1997 and settled in South Florida.

When Yndamiro Restano, the celebrated independent journalist, was released from prison, and the independent journalists came together to form the umbrella group called the Buro de Prensa Independiente, Solano joined, as did Olance's group. CubaPress, another agency that included poet Raul Rivero and Jose Rivero Garcia, chose not to join for fear that a central organization would be too easy for the State to control and destroy. With the formation of the Buro and Yndamiro's travels, the independent journalists gained the attention of several international organizations and received grants from a number of them, including Reporters Without Borders and the Lillian Hellman Foundation.

Unfortunately, the money became a curse. Some journalists pointed fingers at one another with cries of mismanagement. Others felt nonprofessionals were swelling the ranks because they could earn hard currency. Before long, it seemed that the biggest concerns the journalists had were who had mishandled what money and which journalist was being harassed most by the Cuban government, rather than who could do better reporting. The Buro was gutted by these arguments. Yndamiro Restano, the uniting force of the journalists, had wandered far and wide receiving honors and collecting money for the cause, but somewhere along the line he decided that he was not going home to Cuba. Without leadership and suffering State

Security harassment, the Buro foundered and what had seemed to be a hope for a true independent umbrella press organization collapsed. Nevertheless, the Buro, CubaPress, and other small groups continue to file stories that are published in Miami for the U.S. audience or broadcast back to the island by Radio Martí.

< 13 >

The Opposition, Concilio Cubano, and February 24

Out of the night that covers me,
Black as the pit from pole to pole,
I thank whatever gods may be
For my unconquerable soul.

In the fell clutch of circumstance
I have not winced nor cried aloud.
Under the bludgeonings of chance
My head is bloody but unbowed.
—William Ernest Henley

Marta Beatriz Roque, the head of the Association of Independent Economists, is the member of the opposition that I know best. Her comments are scattered throughout this manuscript because I found her to be insightful, thoughtful, and provocative. She is in her forties, has brown hair and fair skin, is keenly intelligent, and is not afraid to speak her mind. I saw her hard at work, reading all she could find about economics and politics, studying English, and researching and writing articles for distribution outside Cuba. She lived in a small apartment in Santo Suarez in a neighborhood that was once working class and lies a fair distance from the center of town. On one of my visits to her home, the power went out, and we sat chatting in the stifling ninety-degree heat with no fan. Her work provided an alternate perspective to that of the State on the Cuban economy and earned her recognition overseas. She published articles in U.S. newspapers and journals, and she was interviewed for American television stories about the island. Even though she was threatened with violence and at times feared for her life, she went on, because she believed in what she was doing. In July 1997, Marta Beatriz was arrested. She was held without trial until March 1999. At that time, she and three of her colleagues were tried in a closed court on charges of sedition. She was sentenced to three and a half years in prison.* I have heard that her health has deteriorated. Given the horrendous conditions of Cuban prisons, I fear for her life.

There is no organized "Opposition" in Cuba. When I refer to the opposition, I am writing about a small number of people who are members of a variety of groups that, despite all odds, oppose the monolithic regime of Fidel Castro. These loosely structured organizations are considered illegal. Being a member of the opposition is not an endeavor for the timid or the weak of convictions. As mentioned in Chapter 1, Cubans who actively oppose the regime are few in number and face great obstacles. Actively dissenting is very difficult, for the rewards are few and the penalties are many. Those who openly disagree with the regime face harassment and often imprisonment. These people, however, do not have to live with the *doble moral*. They live as they believe. They are like a voice crying the truth in a wilderness of enforced silence.

The individuals drawn to the opposition are black, white, and mulatto. They are men and women, young and old. They are educated, thinking people. They do not necessarily agree on what is right for the island, but they know that change is needed. Most of them also look up to Gustavo Arcos, perhaps the best known of the activists and head of the Cuban Committee for Human Rights. He was once a revolutionary and very close to Fidel. In fact, he was with Fidel during the historic attack on the Moncada barracks. In the early years of the regime, he was Cuba's ambassador to Belgium. He found himself facing problems, however, when he began to question the authoritarian nature of the regime. He has been imprisoned twice, once in the late 1960s and again in the early 1980s. The organization he leads tries to inform people about the Universal Dec-

* Her associates Felix Bonne and Rene Gomez Manzano were sentenced to four years each, and Vladimiro Roca was sentenced to five years.

laration of Human Rights and shares information on human rights violations on the island with international organizations.

Gustavo Arcos is at the helm of the opposition, whether or not there is a unifying organization. He is the one to whom the younger people go for advice. His manner is tranquil, and he seems to be at peace with himself. He is measured in his comments, philosophical, and considered to be a man of honor.

Most opposition groups on the island have just a handful of members, but a few, like Arcos's group, claim a hundred or more participants. In addition to the groups dedicated to human rights, there are organizations of independent economists, doctors, and lawyers. They challenge people to take a different look at Cuba, not just to accept what the State declares to be true. Human rights groups keep track of the rights abuses that occur on the island, while the independent economists use their talents to analyze and rebut State economic reports. Some groups write pieces for Miami newspapers; others grant interviews. The work of the opposition is not easy. Because there is so little paper and no access to printing presses, much less copy machines, many on the island are not familiar with the names or the messages of the dissident community. When they wish to share ideas, members of opposition groups do so verbally or pass banned books from hand to hand. Occasionally, fax machines and computers make their way to the island, but the watchful eye of the State misses little, so the houses are searched and the machines are confiscated.

Although potentially thousands in Cuba support the ideas of the opposition, many who might join are afraid to take the risk of losing what little they have. Others are discouraged because they see the effort as quixotic, an attempt to fight a battle that cannot be won. Why take the risk of going to prison or being marginalized if nothing will be accomplished by confronting the regime? In addition, since the time Fidel took power, many of the people who did not support the system have left the island. The United States has welcomed those seeking refuge and still does under the Cuban Adjustment Act. Given the choice of leaving Cuba or joining a dissident group, most choose the former. If all those who have left the island because they did not support the regime had stayed, the opposition might be much larger.

The State makes every effort to discredit the opposition. It starts by calling the organizations *grupusculos* (little tiny groups) to emphasize the limited number of people involved. Because there are many personalities at play in these groups, they tend to break apart as a result of disagreements and then come together again under a different name with some changes in the membership. Since relatively few Cubans *actively* oppose the regime, the same names keep showing up in these groups. The effervescence of these organizations does not exactly strengthen the opposition.

One of the State's favorite attacks is to claim the *grupusculos* are being funded by "Miami terrorist organizations." Despite this accusation, little money comes to dissident groups from Miami. Independent economist Marta Beatriz Roque put the claim in perspective when she said, "If they had given us half the money they claim to have given, we would all be millionaires. Instead, look at us." Although some groups do receive a few thousand dollars a year from international human rights foundations, most dissidents live hand to mouth. They have been thrown out of their jobs, so they must depend on the support of friends and family.

Another way the Cuban government tries to undermine the opposition is by infiltrating the groups. A group often becomes aware of an infiltrator when privately discussed information becomes known to State Security. The State's presence seems to be everywhere. On one occasion, a foreigner who had left money and a computer with members of opposition groups was questioned by State Security as he was leaving Cuba. The authorities knew who he was and how much money he had left with each person he had visited. No one is ever certain who the infiltrators are, so within the groups disputes arise over accusations that one person or another is a State Security informant. The people in these groups know the importance of unity; often those fomenting disruption are actually the people working for State Security.

In October 1995, the opposition groups decided that they needed to put aside their differences and come together under an umbrella organization. Over 130 groups united in what became known as Concilio Cubano. The members focused on the views they had in common. Their founding statement expressed their support for several goals, including a nonviolent transition toward a democratic society, unconditional amnesty for all political prisoners, and legal changes that would secure respect for all universally recognized human rights. Attempts had previously been made to unite the opposition, but this time the groups had a goal: a large meeting to be held on February 24 to discuss the future of Cuba.

Concilio Cubano was born on the island; it was not an idea that came from abroad. In fact, some of the groups that had connections in Miami had to persuade their stateside partners that Concilio was a positive step. Though some Miami organizations were slow to acknowledge Concilio, this recognition was not important. The group was already getting attention from the international press, including interest from some journalists who had never before shown an interest in human rights. Visiting European dignitaries and U.S. congressional delegations met with representatives of Concilio. By February, even average Cubans were paying attention, having learned of Concilio through Radio Martí. One morning I talked with three activists, Felix Bonne, Georgina Gonzalez, and Yanez Pelletier, when they dropped by the Interests Section. They were optimistic and radiated a certainty that there was going to be a positive result from the efforts of Concilio Cubano. The passion and dedication these people held for their cause were evident in their eyes.

On February 10, Concilio Cubano elected its governing board. The founding members did not present themselves for election, letting others take the lead. Lionel Morejon Amagro, a dynamic lawyer in his thirties, was elected president. As plans for the February 24 meeting were well underway, a crackdown on the Concilio began on February 15. By the time the State's offensive slowed two weeks later, over 150 people had been detained or harassed. The violent disturbances of August 1994, in contrast, had resulted in only 35 detentions and cases of harassment. Opposition figure Elizardo Sanchez kept a running record of the people affected by the crackdown. For about two weeks there were, on average, two dozen activists in detention. The names changed, but the numbers remained the same. I watched the list for names of people I knew and worried as each was detained. Most were detained for a short period of time and released, but others were detained and held. By February 19, all five of the newly elected members of the secretariat were in detention. Within two days, both the founding members and the remainder of the elected board of the Concilio had given written statements saying the meeting of the Concilio would be postponed. With the announcement of the postponement, it appeared that the situation might be calming down. The people involved with Concilio thought they would be able to regroup and go forward. There was a sense that they had achieved something because they had irritated the government of Cuba. Fidel perceived them as a threat. The events, however, had not yet played out.

February 24, 1996

February 24 began as a quiet Saturday. I went horseback riding in Parque Lenin. On the drive to the park I commented to a colleague, who was also taking riding lessons, that I hoped the day would stay quiet. He responded, "Is there any reason it shouldn't?"

By the end of the afternoon, two Florida-based small airplanes had been shot out of the air over international waters by Cuban MiG fighters. When I learned about the incident, I went to the office, where I found a skeleton crew already at work. We were fully cog-

nizant of the seriousness of the action that launched Havana into
the headlines of newspapers and the front lines of U.S. diplomacy.
The two nations were in conflict. Adrenalin, shock, and questions
permeated the air. The Brothers to the Rescue organization had been
flying small private aircraft over the Florida Straits on a regular ba-
sis since 1991 in an effort to look for rafters. They would drop fresh
water to the rafters and radio the location to the Coast Guard, which
would send a rescue team. With the signing of the migration accords, the numbers of rafters dropped dramatically, but the group
continued to fly relief missions to the Bahamas, where some rafters
were held in camps. Some say that the organization, which began
as a purely humanitarian effort, had become more political and was
trying to provoke opposition to Castro on the island. The Cuban
government complained that these planes would sometimes violate
the island's airspace. The U.S. government warned the pilots not to
enter Cuban airspace, but it could not stop them from flying because of U.S. rights guarantees. Is violating airspace a sufficient reason to shoot down unarmed civilian aircraft? Three Brothers to the
Rescue planes left South Florida that day in February, but only one
returned. Four people died.

The days that followed blurred together. I reached a point where
I did not know what day it was—I just went to work. That first
night was focused on the search and rescue attempt, in the hope
that some trace of the people and craft could be found. The first
Coast Guard plane had seen an oil slick, but no other trace of
wreckage was found. President Clinton spoke on television, announcing to the American people what had happened. Cubans and
Americans alike wondered how the United States was going to respond to the incident. Tension was very high at the mission, because none of us knew what was going to happen. What steps would
the Clinton administration take? Where were we headed? On Mon-
day, the president announced the U.S. response: All charter flights
between the countries were to be eliminated and the personnel at

the Cuban Interests Section in Washington, DC, were to be restricted. The president also said that the United States would take action through international organizations. Secretary of State Madeleine Albright took the case to the UN Security Council and obtained a statement deploring the incident. In a press briefing, Albright made a reference to the widely published transcripts of the communications between the pilots of the two Cuban MiGs. She declared, "Frankly, this is not *cojones*,* this is cowardice." Cuban Foreign Minister Roberto Robaina later responded, "We have never lacked the former and have never exhibited the latter." The most significant and longest lasting step President Clinton took was agreeing to sign the controversial Helms-Burton legislation, which he had once firmly opposed. This bill, supported by conservative Cuban-American groups, imposed tough sanctions on foreign enterprises trading with the island, reinforced the economic embargo, and gave strict guidelines for U.S. policy toward Cuba. Riding on the emotional wave of the downing of the planes, the Helms-Burton legislation sped through the House and Senate to the president's desk.

Some say Fidel miscalculated. I do not think that is the case. He is a very intelligent man and knew what he was doing. Did the United States play into his hands? Quite possibly. Fidel got what he wanted. Helms-Burton was passed, causing problems for the United States with its closest allies. Mexico, Canada, and many European nations, which have trading relationships with the island, are up in arms about the legislation. However, their opposition is not, as Fidel would have us believe, because they support his absolute rule, but rather because they resent the United States for trying to tell them with which countries they can trade. Sadly, because this law has caused such an uproar internationally, the reason for its passage, the attack on unarmed civilian planes, has faded from public con-

* To "have *cojones*" means, colloquially, to have guts, or courage.

sciousness to be replaced by an antagonism toward the United States and its attempt to legislate to the world.

Even though radar trackings and eyewitnesses clearly place the sites of the downings well outside Cuban territorial waters, the Castro government argued that it was acting within its rights. It blamed the United States for allowing the Brothers to the Rescue to fly into its country's airspace and claimed the planes were shot down over Cuban waters. Fidel went so far as to tell *Time* magazine that he had ordered the downing. The Cuban media portrayed the Brothers to the Rescue planes as "pirate airships" that were bent on terrorist actions. The lightweight Cessnas were also described as military aircraft shot down over Cuban territorial waters. State-controlled television showed both Robaina's and Albright's full statements at the United Nations General Assembly, focusing attention on the fact that Robaina received praise after his presentation whereas Albright left alone after hers. The Cuban media criticized the U.S. press coverage, claiming that it did not show the American people the truth because it carried only excerpts of Robaina's and Albright's speeches and did not show the aftermath. The Cuban press showed all of this, so how, it asked, can Cuba be criticized for not telling people the whole story?

This propagandistic barrage was fairly effective. Most Cubans I spoke with believed that, indeed, the planes had been shot down in their airspace, but they also believed that excessive force had been used. Their rendition of the story reflects that they did not accept everything they were told. All lamented the loss of life. The event had an enormous impact on the island because of what it portended. People did not know what suffering was going to befall them next. Only one thing was clear: Fidel would never change. For the months leading up to February 24, visits from overseas relatives and the perceived potential for better relations with the United States had given people a reason to hope their situation might improve. They had been catching glimpses of the light at the end of the tunnel.

When the planes were blown from the sky, that light was snuffed out. The prevailing feelings were despair and a need for continued forbearance.

Although the State had officially expressed its objections to over-flights, the people responded to one of these airborne visits with quite a different attitude. In January 1996, strips of colored paper printed with statements from the Universal Declaration of Human Rights and such comments as "Fear is for the government, not for the people" fell from the sky over San Miguel del Padron, a suburb of Havana. Miguel, a resident of that area, told me, "My neighbor showed me a piece of paper and called me out to the street. The roof of my house was covered with the flyers. They were all over the street. Everyone—adults, children, and even policemen—were running to pick up the leaflets and trying to grab them out of the air." Miguel did not see the airplane that dropped them. The next day at church the leaflets were all anyone was talking about. It was a moment of excitement. An event had broken through the wall that separates Cuba from the rest of the world. That breakthrough gave people a curious optimism that something good was coming. These provoca-tive paper messages from the sky gave them a sense that change was not impossible. They were not moved to rebel, but they became aware that individuals outside Cuba were concerned about their struggles.

Even though leaflets had fallen over a Havana neighborhood and the Cuban government was irritated by the Brothers to the Rescue flights, the Cuban military could have pursued other, less forceful, means of impeding the Cessnas on February 24. Why, after suc-cessfully improving the island's image internationally, would Fidel take such a confrontational course of action? I would say that he had three goals: He had to maintain the specter of the United States as the enemy, he had to divert attention from the activities of Concilio Cubano, and he had to rein in the population, which was gaining some economic independence and beginning to speak openly of

change. Until February 24, there were rumors that U.S-Cuba relations might be improving. The two nations had a working agreement on migration. Congressmen and a variety of delegations were
visiting the island. Academic visitors, including student groups, were
establishing contact with universities. Cubans living abroad were
visiting relatives all over the island, spreading wealth, and inevitably
carrying the influence of the outside world. If this interaction continued, Fidel could lose his scapegoat—the United States and its
economic embargo. Without an external enemy, he would have no
place to put the blame for economic difficulties. When direct flights
between the two countries were halted after the downing of the
planes and emotions against the Castro regime were running high,
the flow of expatriate visitors slowed dramatically, stemming the tide
of money and foreign ideas. In the United States, anything having
to do with Cuba became anathema. Invitations from universities
and private organizations were rescinded. As one person who can-
celed an invitation to an environmentalist said, "Cuba is interesting. The environment is good. Cuba, the environment, and two
planes in the water is bad." The growing people-to-people contact
ended because of the anti-Castro feelings. Cubans were again cut
off from the outside world. By shooting down the Brothers to the
Rescue planes, Fidel brought relations between the United States
and Cuba to what Ricardo Alarcon called the "lowest point since
the Bay of Pigs." A senior American diplomat in Havana who was
not given to exaggeration said to a visiting reporter quite bluntly,
"Relations are bad."

The downing of the planes also drew attention away from the
plight of Concilio Cubano. Because all eyes were on the bilateral
conflict, the focus of interest shifted away from internal difficulties
and the formation of an umbrella organization of opposition groups.
Just as only months before the creation of Concilio had led to a blos-
soming of the number of individuals in the dissident community, the
crackdown on dissent and the shooting down of the planes led to a

mass exodus through the door of the U.S. refugee program. I sat with Marta Beatriz Roque as she assessed what had happened to Concilio. She showed me a list of the participants and said, "It looks like many of them just saw this as a way to leave. Look, this one is gone now, that one is gone, this one is going. Eighty percent of these people have applied for refugee status." The few who remained included the original core group of opposition figures and a handful of others who, like Concilio president Lionel Morejon Amagro, were imprisoned. Concilio, despite the hope and efforts of its members, fell into disarray. By shooting down the planes, Fidel brought the momentum of economic and social change on the island to a grinding halt. There was no doubt who was in charge. The Party Plenum laid out the new militancy of the Party line. There would be no space to think in Cuba.

< 14 >

The Fifth Party Plenum

Requiem for Hope

They are cutting off the heads of anyone who thinks in this country!
—a Cuban professor

Cubans knew, as soon as the planes were shot down, that their political lives were about to become much more difficult. The passage of the Helms-Burton legislation and the escalation of bilateral tensions had an effect on the State. It convoked the fifth Party plenum in the history of the Revolution to determine the strategy for dealing with the change in Cuba's world. The last event that precipitated a plenum was the end of Soviet aid. The plenum was held just days after the passage of the Helms-Burton legislation. Carlos Lage gave the Party's report on the economic situation of the country, which did not evoke a tremendous response from the Cuban people. They were waiting for the other shoe to drop. And drop it did. Raul Castro's speech, the political report of the Party plenum, given March 23, devastated any thinking Cuban.

After years of practice, people on the island know how to decipher the messages of speeches and the newspapers. The morning the speech came out in the newspaper, I was with a group of Cubans as they read the account and, obviously upset, named the people and organizations to which Raul had obliquely referred. The atmosphere was heavy with emotion. The people affected were friends and former colleagues of those who were reviewing the speech with me. Clearly, intellectuals were under attack. One researcher at the Center for the Study of the Americas who had been singled out by the speech had a heart attack that day. Some blamed Raul's speech for his death. The lengthy speech began with an attack on the "monstrous" Helms-Burton law:

> This law does not only mean for Cuba the tightening of the blockade we have suffered for over 35 years, and it is more than an open and declared economic war. It is a detailed, criminal plan of action to make our people surrender out of starvation and disease. This slavery law aims to deceive, confuse, and disarm the elements they consider the most vulnerable within the Cuban population, through an increase in radio propaganda and other means of ideological diversion. . . . With these ingredients, the fascist law is aimed at creating the ideal climate for "humanitarian" military action.

The proper response to this new siege was, of course, Revolutionary fervor and dedication to the ideals of socialism. Those groups seen as damaging ideological devotion to the Revolution included tourists and diplomats. The tourists, Raul said, "in general want to see new things and rest. . . . But it should not be forgotten that since they come from capitalist countries, they bring with them ideas about consumer society." He portrayed the diplomats as much more insidious, saying: "Diplomatic representatives based in the U.S. Interests Section in Havana as well as some officials from other countries [are displaying a] diplomatic lifestyle that has little to do with diplomacy. They are making trips to the provinces to gain information, and penetrating the intellectual world, education, medicine, and the youth . . . trying to create divisions, confusion, and an ideological penetration in order to destabilize us."

Then Raul turned his sights not on the external enemy but on the internal one—those who failed to display complete dedication to the socialist goals of the Revolution—in other words, all those who are not true believers and Party faithful. It was this assault that rocked the island. First in line for criticism were the private farmers and the self-employed, who contributed to the economy but were also making a decent living without the State. According to Raul, "The psychology of private farmers and self-employed in general tends toward individualism and is not a source of socialist consciousness." Not only could the self-employed join the nouveau riche, but they might also become involved in profiteering, could "form groups that are divorced from the State," and could become the "breeding ground for the subversive work of the enemy." The answer, obviously, was for the State to remind them of their status as workers. Those who broke the law were to be severely punished, and taxes were to be high to keep these people from gaining too much profit. Over a year after this speech, the effects were still being felt. The official number of self-employed workers dropped below 200,000. In the face of high taxes, many smaller enterprises closed their doors.

Next in line for the assault were those Party members who, Raul said, "have for some time professed an ideology which is not ours [Fidel's]." In the same breath he condemned those in think tanks who "adopt a passive, complacent, irresponsible attitude in the face of factors which divert them from [the goals of the Revolution]." There was more, but the message was clear. All expression and research could have but one end: support for the Revolution. The speech concluded:

> We have and will continue to have socialism. However, the only form of socialism possible in Cuba today requires us to assimilate . . . certain elements of capitalism and reinsert ourselves into the world economy. . . . As President Fidel Castro has pointed out, such a complex panorama calls for us to fight for our socialist objectives with supreme effort, with sweat, and with a good deal of intelligence. We must follow a cardinal principle when we apply theories dictated by reality: we must maintain our revolutionary purity.*

* "Political Bureau's Report," *Granma International,* April 10, 1996.

The intellectual community was stunned. A speech like the one Raul had given might have been appropriate in the 1960s or early 1970s, but in the 1990s it was an anachronism. Society and circumstances had changed. The same ideological rigidity of the early days of the Revolution could not be asked of people, yet this was what was being demanded. It is difficult to overstate the significance of this speech. For most Cubans, hope for change died with that speech. The pall that it cast over the island still remains. Ideological rigidity is the rule. Variance from that norm has vicious consequences. The brief moment of political openness afforded Cuban thinkers, both those in the opposition and those within the system, ended February 24. The shooting down of the planes and the Fifth Party Plenum reflected a simple truth: There would be no change in Fidel's Cuba. The light at the end of the tunnel was effectively extinguished.

< 15 >

Reminiscing

On Quinta Avenida just beyond the tunnel that links Miramar and Vedado, there is a house that is a metaphor for Cuba. The house is beautiful, with a green tile roof and a turret, a cream-colored facade, and an elegant European design. The roof, however, is falling in, leaving only the turret intact. Windows are broken, and plaster is peeling off the outside walls. Looking through the glass panes of the front door, I could see laundry hung across the foyer. A stained glass window graced the wall behind the wide stairway and a tall antique clock stood to the side. Rumor has it that the elderly woman who lives in the house has refused to move out and give her home to the State. The essence of the house, like that of Cuba, is intact, but the structure that holds it is collapsing. The people, hanging their laundry across the elaborate foyer, are doing what is necessary to survive in the shell of a palace that is no longer a showplace but merely a shelter. No one knows if the house can be saved.

Cubans showing a visitor around Havana will describe everything as it was and little as what it is. The litany may include observations on what building housed the best bakery in the city or where the Canada Dry bottling plant was. "That used to be a Woolworth store," one man told me. "When I was a boy I bought candied apples there." He added that it had been years since he had eaten an apple. He could not afford one. Infanta, a broad avenue, was once a busy shopping and commercial area. Now it is a seemingly endless expanse of empty storefronts. Neon signs from the 1950s still mark some of the long since closed enterprises. Beyond the open doors of the few "stores" still open sit bored clerks with little to sell. Pedestrians walk along the street without even glancing at the storefronts, which once were the delight of window-shoppers. Against this weathered and aging backdrop, one man, dressed in a loose cotton shirt, shorts, and homemade sandals, said, "We Cubans used to be very stylish. People dressed well. Men wore suits and hats. Women followed the latest fashions. Now look at us." While his words capture fleeting memories of a romanticized prerevolutionary Havana, his bitter perception of the current Cuban condition marks the once shining hope of the Revolution as now merely a shell of rhetoric and pain.

Mrs. Rojas will turn ninety this year. Her manners and speech mark her as a true lady, a vision of what was once the best of Cuba. Although she and her husband had come from humble beginnings, they had been able through hard work and talent to raise themselves to considerable prosperity. She and her husband chose not to leave when Fidel took power, because her husband felt he was too old to start over in a new country. With the Revolution, they lost all of their holdings save one small rental house. She still lives on the first floor of that house, surrounded by Limoges china and Baccarat crystal, French porcelain figurines, and family photographs. The top floor she rents out for income. She does not support Fidel. I doubt she ever has. She believes Fidel has made a travesty of her nation.

Mrs. Rojas does not go out any longer. "Why should I?" she asked, focusing her blue eyes on me. "I do not know anyone here anymore. All my friends went to the United States." As we wandered through her house, she said, "This is my world. This is where my memories are." She proudly showed me her 1920s wedding portrait and more recent photographs of her grandchildren in the United States. She was up-to-date on world events and occasionally spoke English with me. Her elegance and grace are a symbol of what a Cuban lady was. She invited me to join her for afternoon tea. We sat together at her lace-covered dining table, just as we might have forty years before, and sipped tea from Limoges cups.

PART II   The Cuban Spirit

< 16 >

Soy Cuba

I Am Cuba

Great men, great nations, have not been boasters and buffoons, but perceivers of the terror of life, and have manned themselves to face it.
—Ralph Waldo Emerson

Soy Cubano. No puedo ser diferente.
(I am Cuban. I can't be anything else.)
—José Martí

The Cuban reality is painful. The constant struggle to get by economically drains people of energy. The political situation, with its constraints on expression and action, prevents individuals from changing their lives. The very survival of people in this environment seems surreal. How do Cubans face the adversity of each day? How have they survived watching the country they love fall to ruin? How have they confronted the bankruptcy of the Revolution and coped as they saw the better future they were building collapse? How do they go on, knowing there is no way out and possibly not even a way through?

The answer embodies, perhaps, the essence of being Cuban. Despite tremendous adversity, or because of it, the spirit of Cuba has survived and grown strong. The people of the island are bound together in a web of life. Friends and family make life bearable. People nurture and care for one another. Because material goods are scarce, most have learned that human niceties, such as a kind word or touch, are what is truly essential. These people have not merely survived; they continue to give one another love and have not lost their joy for life. This humanity and willingness to help one another have kept the society from falling apart.

A U.S. Coast Guard captain in charge of one of the cutters that repatriated rafters told me he respected Cubans because of his experiences rescuing them on the high seas during the rafter crisis of August 1994. In the early morning darkness he could make out a few rafts. As the dawn broke, he realized that there were literally hundreds of rafts floating on the waves. He had rescued people leaving other islands and had noticed that often the strongest would scramble out of the boats first. With the Cubans, he said, it was different. "The raft could be sinking, but they would lift out the women and children first, then the old men, and then the young men would come. There was a sense of responsibility. They took care of each other."

Because they have so many difficulties, people have learned to rely on their friends for help. There is no way to meet the emotional and physical demands of life without caring for others and also being cared about. Friends will often come together to help someone in need, as several women I knew did when an eighty-year-old woman became quite ill and was hospitalized. The elderly lady's daughter, the most likely caregiver, had just left on a long awaited vacation out of the country. The news of the mother's illness spread rapidly among the daughter's friends, who stepped in to help before she was even contacted. They took turns visiting the elderly woman in the hospital and brought her meals to her. They felt strongly that their friend should not cut her trip short, especially since they could help. One of the caretakers said, "If it were my mother, my friend would do the same for me."

The help that is offered might be economic or material as well. When a baby is expected, friends, neighbors, and relatives will collect scarce items that will help the expectant parents, from a crib to baby clothes. One woman with brown hair, fair skin, and intelligent brown eyes spoke to me with affection for her family in another town, saying that she wanted to do more for them, despite her limited resources. "When my husband died," she said, "my cousins helped me with money when they could and with lots of love. Now they have almost nothing. It is so sad—they once had jobs and were doing well. Now they have nothing. They cannot afford shoes for their daughter so she can go to school. I try to send money when I can, but I have four children."

The helping hand is offered to foreigners as well. On the rafter monitoring trip I took to the eastern end of the island, my colleague and I received some of that freely given aid. On our way out of Santiago, we made a wrong turn and had to turn around. Unfortunately, in the process of correcting our mistake, we managed to get our vehicle stuck in a ditch. We had no idea how we were going to get ourselves out of the situation. To our pleasant surprise, we had no sooner gotten stuck when a group of Cubans in a van traveling in the opposite direction stopped and helped lift the jeep out of the ditch. They asked where we were headed and then helped us find the unmarked turn to our destination. They left us with waves and smiles.

It is not just in crises that the best of the human spirit emerges. Everyday occurrences are laced with affection. In Cuba, the personal is very important. The first courtesy is to ask how someone is and not expect a one-word answer. Individuals ask each other about their families and offer cups of coffee. Perhaps because there are no goods to buy and there are shortages of everything, people have learned to give of themselves. Cubans visit one another. They just drop in. Meals are shared. Those who may not have food are welcomed at others' tables. The favor is repaid somehow. They are part of one another's lives. Everyone knows if someone is sick or in need or in love. Relationships with family and friends are the basic elements of life. These connections make Havana seem like a small town. People went to school together, are in-laws, or worked together. The community is a tightly knit network. For one party at my home, I invited a particularly diverse group including artists, journalists, religious people, and academics. I was surprised at how many knew each other. Two had fought together against Batista and had been close friends ever since. One had taught another man's child. Another two had worked in television together. Interconnections link people across the city and across the island.

Cubans spend a lot of time outside, sitting on their front steps or balconies, walking to school or work, or just standing in line for rationed items. Not only do they enjoy the fresh air, but they see their neighbors and chat with one another. Signs of life are everywhere in Havana's neighborhoods. The early morning hours are quiet, but as the rising sun hits the tops of the trees, life begins. A Lada rambles by, then two bicycles pass by as I walk my dog. A rooster crows. Down the block, a thin elderly black man is already on his streetside stool, ready to watch the world go by. I wave; he returns the wave and smiles. Soon the neighborhood is wide awake with children going to school and adults going to work on bicycles. Music with a pulsing Latin beat is almost always playing, either at the bar next door or on a radio in one of the apartment buildings, giving an underlying rhythm to life. The evenings contain a mixture of sounds that reflect the life all around me: a baby crying, birds singing, the voice of a father with his toddler, an impromptu baseball game on the street, a truck rumbling by, a rooster crowing. The cacophony is pleasant and most definitely alive.

There are rhythms that are uniquely Cuban. Afro-Cuban music, sung in the Yoruba language, has a pulsing vitality that seems linked to the rhythm of life on the island. I was first swept away by these rhythms in Santiago, in, of all places, the hotel on San Juan Hill (a location that is famous for Teddy Roosevelt's charge). The neighbor and the son-in-law of the playwright Ana Maria were performing with a group and invited me and a friend to come watch. In the side courtyard of the hotel, under towering trees and the stars, we were treated to an evening of song and dance that was far closer in style to Nigeria than to Madrid. Drums, other percussion instruments, a lone saxophone, and voices provided the sensual music that wove a magic spell around the audience and performers. The woman we knew, Damaris, sang the first number and directed her wiles toward my friend COB Blaha. Later she pulled me out to the dance floor to do the merengue with one of the band members. A woman dressed as a sexy Tropicana dancer in a tiny *tanga* performed a provocative solo dance, and a group of eight men and women in brightly colored costumes danced a precision number wearing sandals that made loud clapping sounds. At the end of the show, the cast and half the audience danced and formed into a conga line. There was a vibrant energy to the music and the evening.

Cubans seek release from their worries, and though alcoholism may be increasing, there is a more popular outlet in music and dancing. When there is a party, everyone contributes. It is almost as if food magically appears. The parable of the loaves and fishes seems to occur daily in this land of scarcity where people who have almost nothing are somehow able to produce enough to share. A bit of bravado may be needed, but a cake and even party favors can be found for a birthday party. When my friend Lucrecia decided to give her husband, Orlando, a surprise party for his sixtieth birthday, she knew that obtaining the cake would be a challenge. The State provides birthday cakes only for children up to twelve years old. Lucrecia went to the bakery and told the gentleman that she wanted to order a birthday cake. The exchange went something like this:

"Certainly, just bring in the child's identity card which shows he is under twelve and you can pick up your cake."

"Well . . . the child is actually my husband who is turning sixty. I am throwing him a surprise party." The man burst out laughing.

"No one has ever told me a story like that. I'll tell you what. Bring in your husband's identity card that shows he is turning sixty, and I will get you that birthday cake."

The birthday party was complete with a cake, a piñata, and children's games.

For Thanksgiving 1995, I attended a party at the home of an American, where more than half the guests were Cuban. After the food was all eaten—and I mean all—a musician named Eduardo sat at the piano and began to play songs. He played pop tunes and songs from Broadway musicals, and the Cubans sang. When Ramon Fabian Veloz, a young singer of the Cuban country music called Guajira, joined the singing, the music switched to traditional songs. People sang along and a few began to dance. After several songs, one of the guests, Celina Gonzalez, the queen of Guajira music, who must be near seventy, stood and began to sing. She was dressed in her trademark style, a lacy long-sleeved and high-necked blouse and a flowing dark purple skirt. She entranced the crowd, for her presence is dynamic and her music stirring. She sang her famous song "A Santa Bárbara" ("To Saint Barbara") that includes a rousing chorus of "Que viva Changó," saluting an important deity of Santeria. When she performed "Guantanamera," she improvised on the verses to give messages to her audience and thanks to the hostess. Cubans and Americans alike joined her on the chorus. Here was a magic, a glimpse of the joy of Cuba.

Throughout the time I was in Cuba, I found that where there was a piano, there was music and singing. Where there was recorded music, there was dancing—playful, spirited, and unself-conscious. Parties were celebrations. I passed many a wonderful evening dancing with Cubans willing to help me with the rhythm of salsa. At one party, a few of the women had watched me dancing the merengue and took it upon themselves to teach me a few of the sexy moves the Cuban women make when they dance. By the time I was shimmying, we were ready to erupt into gales of laughter. These moments of laughter, music, dancing, and fun are what make it possible to survive the other times. People forget their worries for a few hours and live with great joy. As one professional woman said to me at a beach party on a beautiful day, "Just one day like this of sunshine and good fun and food can make it possible to get through all the other days. If you can really enjoy moments like this, you can survive the rest."

Margarita, a mulatta who is battling breast cancer, embodies the joy for life. To celebrate her saint day, that of the Virgen de la Caridad del Cobre and Ochún, she threw a party for her friends and neighbors. I was the only foreigner there. She and a few friends cleaned the house and prepared a huge pot of soup. People attending the party all contributed something, from beer to rum to foodstuffs. Music was playing and people began to dance. Margarita was the center of it all, being the hostess, laughing, dancing, flirting with her former suitors, and embracing life. The outside world was left behind for a few hours of revelry. Margarita, despite her critical health problems, put her own concerns aside, gave of herself, and found joy in spite of pain. She is not just Cuban, she is Cuba.

< 17 >

Spirit and Soul

When the world is storm-driven and the bad that happens and the worse that threatens are so urgent as to shut everything else from view, then we need to know all the strong fortresses of the spirit which have been built through the ages.—Edith Hamilton

Self-reliance, the height and perfection of man, is reliance on God.
—Ralph Waldo Emerson

Their joy for life and sense of community are part of the reason Cubans have survived and kept their spirit intact. For most visitors to the island, the Cubans' passion for life and consideration of others are evident. But these elements are not the whole story. They may actually be a product of a much more powerful force: faith.

Faith is holding the soul of Cuba together.

Appreciating the powerful role of spirituality is the key to understanding and truly loving the island. Cubans are mystical, magical people. They accept the existence of a world beyond the visible one. Believing there is another world, an existence beyond this one, makes it easier to suffer the trials of this life. The spiritual world is, for them, intrinsically linked to the visible one.

When not viewed through a spiritual lens, what is happening on the island seems surreal. However, once an observer is aware of the spiritual side of the island, an added layer of meaning appears, for the signs of faith are abundant: A professor shows a small gold-colored stone from the town of Cobre, the home of Cuba's patron saint, which she carries as an amulet for good luck and protection. Two mulatto men sitting on a park bench are not just conversing. The older one, a spiritual wise man, is advising the younger, reverently attentive man on how to improve his life. The vegetable seller is dressed in white from head to toe because she has become an initiate in Santeria. The cardinal gives the mass, and the church is filled to overflowing. People pray. Whether to the pantheon of Santeria or to the God of Abraham and Isaac, most people call on the help of higher powers. God and the Holy Spirit are very much alive in Cuba, as are Obbatalá and Changó.

The island is a mystical place. The sea, the exotic tropical plants, the fragrant night-blooming flowers, and the stars that shine on a backdrop of dark blue velvet contribute to a sense of wonder. The sea, and its seemingly infinite expanse, draws Cubans. While it is a source of food and fun, the sea is also a place of contemplation and peace. Along the seawall of the Malecón, there are always people gazing out to sea. They might be just passing time, but it might be something more. One evening my friend Carlos said, "Could you do me a favor? Could we go to the Malecón? I need to see the sea. I need to find some peace." When individuals are facing problems and cannot seem to find a solution, others will advise them to go to the sea. Gazing at the blue water and sky touched by the sun, people can let go of worries as they become more aware of powers that are greater than the individual. One evening I walked down to the coast, just a few blocks from my home, sat on a wall of what was once a swimming area, and stared out at the sea. I was not alone in my reverie. There were two or three other people scattered within a few hundred yards. Each of us was looking out in solitude, seeking peace and understanding. As I became calm and cleared my mind, only taking in the beauty, I felt myself a part of the scene. I was no longer on the island, or even constrained by my body. I was at one with the sea and the sky. I had found a sanctuary—the same sanctuary many Cubans find when they contemplate the sea and all that is greater than they are.

During my time in Cuba, I never heard anyone say that God had forsaken the island. Instead, I heard many references to the fact that the survival of the Cuban people was a miracle. Cubans admit they could not have survived without God. This admission is remarkable considering that until this decade, religious faith was a black mark on one's Revolutionary credentials. Party members could not be religious. In 1991, the Communist Party Congress opened the Party to believers, probably because the growth in Catholicism and Santeria was already evident. For years, the only religion had been Revolution. But as people realized that the socialist dream they had believed in and sacrificed for was only an illusion, they needed something to believe in—some greater power or greater good. With people finding strength in the traditional institutions of the Catholic and Protestant churches or in the more mystical pursuits of *espiritismo* (spiritualism) and Afro-Cuban religions, faith came back with a fervor. Catholicism, *espiritismo,* and Santeria are intimately linked with the island's history and culture. So, while finding religious fulfillment, Cubans are finding their heritage as well.

The Christian religions, both Catholic and Protestant, help Cubans face their dire circumstances by bringing the promise of a better life in the next world and giving hope of resurrection. One Baptist minister likened the Cubans' current situation to the dark times surrounding the death of Christ. But he argued that there would be a resurrection. This hope was reflected in the words of a journalist who commented to me, "I believe Cuba has a great future. We will be like the Asian tigers. We will be one day an economic miracle." Instead of promising a better world in the future, the more mystical traditions of *espiritismo* and the Afro-Cuban faiths put Cubans in touch with the next world—a spiritual world—today. Besides the reassurance that there is life beyond this one, *espiritistas* and *babalaos* (high priests of Santeria), through their contacts with the spiritual world, give people hope and direction for their lives. Both offer insights into just about every aspect of life, from health to romance.

Cubans are not often just Catholic or Protestant or Espiritista or Santero. These paths are entwined. Most people mix Catholicism or Protestantism with one of the mystical traditions. This way, they have both the promise of a better life in the next world and contact in the present with the "*más allá*" (the other side). No matter what path of belief individual Cubans choose, they pursue it with a tremendous faith—a faith that helps them find a solution to the seemingly hopeless situation they face. The strength found in faith is the source of the Cuban capacity to withstand adversity. Just as Americans might pray for health believing in God's ability to work miracles, Cubans also pray for miracles. They have, after all, already seen one. They have survived.

Cuban Catholicism and Protestantism

The Catholic church is more for Cubans than a religious institution. Today it is an educator, a social worker, and a harbor from the madness of daily life. Young people are coming to the Catholic church today not only to find something to believe in and a direction in their lives but also to find a sense of history. They have known nothing but Revolution. While they might be well informed about Soviet history, their knowledge of their own nation's past consists of only what the Revolution found convenient to tell them. The Catholic church has taken on this daunting task of teaching history. This role for the church makes sense, considering the integral part the church has played in Cuban heritage. Catholicism came to the island with Columbus and was nurtured under Spanish colonialism. From the cathedral in Havana Vieja that was completed in 1777 to the chapels in the seventeenth-century fortresses built to protect the harbors in Santiago de Cuba and Havana to the more modern and imposing churches on Quinta Avenida, the architecture reflects how the church and the country are entwined. The Catholic church is addressing present needs by distributing donated goods and medicines through its charity Caritas, by publishing magazines that pro-

vide a small outlet for independent thought, and by running programs to help people overcome alcoholism.

The Catholic church enjoys enormous popularity. When Cardinal Jaime Ortega gives the mass, the church is filled to overflowing.
Many Cubans will go to church each day to pray, whether for the
souls of their misguided Communist Party relatives or for a few more
days of survival. Although it is the only truly independent organization on the island, the Catholic church does not play the role the
church did in Poland of being an opposition force. Yet it will occasionally make its political voice heard, as it did in 1996 when it
clashed with the State over the shooting down of the planes and the
crackdown on Concilio Cubano.

The church is, in many ways, the conscience of the island. The
Conference of Catholic Bishops issues statements that are like a reality check for the State, putting into words some difficult truths
about what is happening in Cuba. For example, after the migration
accord was signed, one of these statements asked that the reasons underlying migration be addressed. The bishops wrote the following:

> What has happened in Cuba? The economic crisis is quite evi-
> dent, and in these situations, many want to find a quick way to
> improve the conditions of their lives. But there is something more
> worrisome, which manifests itself most in the thinking sectors of
> society. There is discontent which is not fundamentally political,
> but can include politics. It is a type of existential discontent. . . .
>
> The fundamental equality of all men and women, of every con-
> dition, whether young or old, sick or healthy, productive or un-
> productive, based on the intrinsic dignity of the human being,
> created by God in his image, is not the same as "egalitarianism."
> This "egalitarianism" is an artificial leveling which places in the
> same category, as far as type of work, vacation, and salary, the doc-
> tor who saves the life of a patient in open heart surgery as the ma-
> chine operator in a textile mill.

When this happens, those most creative sectors of society, the builders of society, do not feel valued and live continually discouraged. So they look for work contracts in any other country, they leave and do not come back. They were not unemployed in Cuba, and often they were the best at their jobs, but they did not conform.

The writer, artist, creator, the entrepreneurial man with technical, commercial, or even scientific abilities looks not only for remuneration appropriate to his skills and production, he also wants to work freely, in a space open to his creativity and its possibilities. But instead he finds limits and difficulties. I am talking here about the internal "blockade" which also disheartens people and makes many wish to leave.[1]

These issues are fundamental in Cuba. The talented and intellectual people are in a difficult position, not permitted to work and think freely and also not compensated for the work they do. The bishops' message was one the State had to hear, but even more important, it was what Cubans needed to hear. The church is speaking aloud the realities of the island. Although high levels of the Catholic church may not openly confront the regime, the church is providing a space for those who are working for change through faith. In fact, in the May 1996 issue of the Catholic magazine *Vitral*, which is published in Cuba, Padre Manuel H. de Cespedes Garcia Menocal wrote:

> The church ought to create space for dialogue, prayer, reflection, and ecclesiastical communion between Christians of different ideological lines. It ought to promote political vocation in the laity, respecting its autonomy in concrete secular actions. . . . The church has a serious responsibility to help form politically all its members so that each one assumes, according to his own situation, the obligation to serve the community. For some this may include meeting in groups or political parties to renew evangelically the

current politics, and to seek, obtain, maintain, and exercise political power.[2]

Some priests and lay people are in fact taking an active role in the future direction of the country through their participation in activities related to the church. Padre Jose Conrado of Palma Soriano and Dagoberto Valdés of Pinar del Río are two such men who are making a difference on the island. Catholic priest Padre Jose Conrado is a man of God. He has a smiling, cherubic face, a stocky body, and a spirit that radiates joy and love. He leads a congregation in the town of Palma Soriano near Santiago de Cuba on the eastern end of the island. The State does not like him very much because he gives people hope. He has gone so far as to read from his pulpit an open letter to Fidel Castro calling for reform. When he completed the letter, in a show of support for him, his parishioners burst into an emotional rendition of the Cuban national anthem. He does not seem to have any fear of the State. He said to me, "What will they do? Throw me in jail? Fine. It has been a while since we have had a priest in jail. I would go."

At my home one evening over dinner, as Padre Jose Conrado was talking about his work, he said, "People are being indoctrinated to believe they cannot change things. I am teaching them they can." Despite the suffering he sees every day, he is optimistic. "I see flowers beginning to bloom," he observed. "I do not believe the State can control the spirit of the people." He told me of one university dean who was asked to do something questionable but declined and said, "I cannot do that." The dean's superior reminded him that he was part of the Communist Party. He responded, "I am also Catholic, and my faith teaches me not to lie." The next week he was removed from his position as a dean with full fanfare and praise for the good job he had done. He was then returned to his former teaching position at the university. In another case the priest told me about, a high-level member of the Communist Youth Union was being berated for attending Padre Jose Conrado's church. The young man took out his Party card and threw it on the table saying, "This is bullshit!" The provincial level of the Communist Youth wanted to throw him out of the organization, but the local level voted against the higher body and supported their colleague.

On the other end of the island, in Pinar del Río, layman Dagoberto Valdés is teaching classes in civics, reminding people what it means to be a Cuban and a citizen. The director of the Catholic Center for Religious and Civic Formation, he recognizes the need for a civil society in Cuba, and in an essay published in 1994 he put forward his hope to "change at the same time hearts and structures." He said, "Do not stay with the sterile complaints and the useless laments about the current situation in Cuba, but rather help us lift the pessimism and discouragement with hope. Hope placed in Him who is God the Father." Dagoberto Valdés is also the director of the magazine *Vitral*. Published by the bishopric of Pinar del Río, the magazine celebrated its third anniversary with the 1997 May-June issue. *Vitral* includes poetry, commentary on social and historical issues, art, articles on human rights, and philosophical and religious pieces. It is a surprise on the landscape of Cuban publications because of its openness and powerful message. Dagoberto has a peace about him, a certainty of his work, and a dedication to Cuba and to God.

Protestant churches play a similar but lesser role to that of the Catholic church. Instead of tracing their roots to Spain, however, the Protestant churches are a result of the long relationship between the United States and Cuba. Baptist, Methodist, and even Quaker churches are found on the island. Recently, evangelical churches have emerged, and charismatic ministers like Orson Villa can attract hundreds of followers. As one would expect, Villa's large following made him a threat, so he was imprisoned by the State. The evangelical churches are growing and, with their charismatic tendencies, are attracting practitioners of Santeria and *espiritismo* as converts.

The State is not quite sure what to do with religion. The great

Christmas tree debate was a sign of the internal divide on this issue. For many years, Christmas decorations were not available at any price, for the religious holiday was not to be celebrated or recognized. In December 1995, Fidel was out of the country, and the mice started playing. The dollar store sold artificial Christmas trees, which disappeared from the shelves almost immediately. At first, trees were appearing in the hotels and tourist locations, but then they started to show up at the *bodegas* and State-run institutions. The situation was too much for the powers that be, and all decorations were banned. Finally, it was decided that ventures catering to foreigners could display such items, but State enterprises, symbols of the socialist ideal, could not.

Far more revealing of the uneasy coexistence of Fidel's regime and Catholicism was the visit by Pope John Paul II to the island in January 1998. The State knew it could gain international status through the visit, especially if the pope condemned the U.S. embargo. That advantage had to be balanced, however, with the challenge to the Castro regime presented by the pope's messages to the Cuban people and by the acknowledgment of the power of religion. Although the foreign press heralded the event as a sign that political change was coming to Cuba, the most important result of the visit was that it gave people a moment of hope. When the pope arrived, devout Catholics and curious onlookers alike filled the streets along his route. One layman, who was thrilled by the visit, told me:

The pope's message was courageous and pertinent to our problems—it was almost as if he had lived in Cuba. He is an extraordinary man. He spoke about the family, youth, the dignity of man, and addressed the issues that affect us. He said that we should follow what Martí said about building a homeland with all Cubans and for the good of all Cubans. I went to see him at the Plaza—it was the first spontaneous gathering there in the last forty years. They say that almost a million people were there. More important than the numbers, though, was the atmosphere of respect that existed between the believers and the nonbelievers. Every comment the pope made about freedom and the dignity of man was applauded by *everyone!* The crowd even chanted slogans like "The pope, free, wants us all to be free!" (*El papa, libre, nos quiere a todos libres*) and "The pope, our friend, Cuba is with you!"

Whatever role the church chooses to play, religious faith—not the Party or the State—has become the rock to which most Cubans cling.

The Mystical Traditions

Espiritismo

Espiritismo, the Cuban variant of spiritualism, has been practiced on the island for over a century. Practitioners, who in the United States are called mystics, mediums, or psychics, are called *espiritistas* in Havana. They are quite sought after for their insights. Those who believe in *espiritismo* hold that all of us have guardian spirits who help and guide us in our lives. The *espiritistas'* contact with the world of these spirits comes through their faith in God. Through visual or auditory communications with the "*más allá*," the *espiritistas* intuit things about the future and past of the people they meet. They also may make predictions about future events, be they political events or natural disasters. In August 1996, two mystics predicted that a natural disaster like a hurricane would hit Cuba that year. The prediction was unusual because Cuba, unlike many Caribbean islands, had not been hit directly by a hurricane in many years. One of the *espiritistas* went so far as to say the storm would strike the island in mid-October. Hurricane Lili pounded the island on October 17, 1996.

The modern beginning of spiritualism is considered to have occurred in the United States, at the home of the Fox family in Hydesville, New York, in 1848. For several weeks, mysterious knocks were heard on the wall in the room where two girls were sleeping. The girls were frightened and moved to their parents' room. Gradually, the family became braver and started clapping and knocking back. The knocks responded. Before long the knocker answered questions. Many people came to the house and witnessed this phenomenon, a direct encounter with the spirit world.[3]

By the second half of the nineteenth century, popular spiritualism was spreading across America, and Europe as well, where Alan Kardec, a Frenchman, wrote books on spiritualism that later appeared in Cuba. It is uncertain what route spiritualism took to the island, but it arrived there around the middle of the nineteenth century, coinciding with the beginning of the independence movement.[4] Because it arrived at that time, it became linked with the desire for independence and thereby with the Cuban experience. It continues to be part of life on the island because the *espiritistas,* with their psychic and clairvoyant abilities and their insight into human nature, give spiritual advice to people, helping them to deal with the demands of life under Fidel.

Most *espiritistas* have their first mystical experience by the age of five or six, dreaming about future events or having visions. Children in the United States have these experiences as well, but Americans tend to ignore these happenings or are puzzled by them. Cubans, in contrast, consider the ability to be God-given and will sometimes take such children to a teacher who can help them develop their skills. Among the people I knew, several acknowledged that they had the gift of *espiritismo* but had never developed it. One showed me a pendant that was given to her to protect her from the "*mala vista,*" or evil eye. Another told me this story:

My husband died sixteen years ago in an automobile accident, and I never remarried. People have told me they can sense my husband all around me, that his spirit is closely attached to mine.

I feel his presence sometimes. I am an *espiritista,* as were my mother and grandmother. I am from Oriente [the eastern end of the island], and *espiritismo* is very strong there. I have never been trained—I am too afraid. After my husband's death, a friend from out of town who is an *espiritista*, who had not come to the funeral, came to visit. One morning she asked, "Was your husband wearing a red plaid shirt and light brown pants when he was buried?" "Well, yes," I said, "he was." She said, "Last night I saw him sitting on the end of the bed looking at your sons."

When *espiritistas* do a formal reading or spiritual mass, they will sit with others at a table on which there is some combination of candles, flowers, a glass of water, a crucifix, and incense. They recite the Lord's Prayer and the Apostles' Creed, focus, and achieve a higher spiritual state. If they are doing just a quick psychic reading, the accoutrements often are not needed, just concentration. Some of the simpler practices, like leaving a glass of water out for the spirits, are copied by believers. Not surprisingly, even the spiritual realm of life is not immune from the jokes of the Special Period. As one irreverent soul commented, "Be careful not to use water from the tap to fill the glass; use distilled water. If you don't, considering the water these days, you might get a bad case of spiritual diarrhea." All joking aside, in many households there is a glass of water placed on a high shelf to draw the good spirits.

One evening, Juan, a man with cinnamon skin and large brown eyes, invited me to go to dinner at a *paladar* that a friend of his owned. The small restaurant was in the backyard of a home, and the clientele were all peso-earning Cubans. As soon as we sat down, the owner arrived with drinks and a plate of food for us—at no charge. A few moments later a woman came over to our table and joined us. She started chatting with my friend, and then she asked for spiritual advice. After her departure, only a few minutes passed before a middle-aged man approached us and sat down. He was troubled with family problems and came to my friend for guidance. At the restaurant, Juan was a well-known figure. He was a respected *espiritista*. For those who believe, advice from mystics is perceived as divinely inspired counsel. The insights that are shared give people guideposts and markers for their life, solutions to problems, and hope for the future.

The other Cubans who deal with the spirit world, but from a different perspective, are the *babalaos* of Santeria.

Santeria

The Afro-Cuban religions touch many aspects of life on the island and are followed by individuals of all races. There are three major Afro-Cuban religious traditions, Santeria, or Regla de Ocha, which has its origin with slaves from Yoruba areas spanning from Ghana to the Niger valley; Palo Monte, which has its roots with Bantu tribes from the Congo; and the Secret Society of the Abakua, which originated with a group of escaped slaves and free blacks who worked to liberate those who were still slaves. Most of this section addresses the predominant tradition of Santeria.

The popularity of Afro-Cuban religions on the island is not new. Before the Revolution, Santeria was already an ingrained part of the culture. Many white households had nannies or maids who were black and brought with them the folklore, so nearly everyone had some exposure to it. Today, even the most devout Catholics sometimes find themselves placing white or red flowers in their houses, for either Obbatalá or Changó.

Santeria is a blending of African religion with the Catholic faith. A pantheon of African deities was melded with the array of saints of Spanish Catholicism. For those who believe in the Afro-Cuban religions, a significant part of the population, there is no conflict between Santeria and Catholicism. It is like an addition. References to Santeria are part of the language and culture. If a person is having bad luck, friends will say, often in jest, that the unfortunate soul needs to see a *babalao*, a high priest of Santeria. The assumption implied in the comment is that a bad spirit or unhappy *orisha* (god) is plaguing the person. A *babalao* can tell the person how to appease the spirit and solve the problem. In the Yoruba language, *babalao* means "father," so a priest of Santeria has the same title as a priest of the Catholic church.[5]

When Africans were taken to Cuba as slaves, they brought their religion with them. Most of the slaves came from West Africa. There, the gods were ancestors who had power. These deities, however, could not manifest themselves unless they possessed one of their descendants. Each village had its own gods, which were ancestors of those in the village, but there were also certain powerful ones, such as Obbatalá, that were found throughout West Africa. The various deities watched over different aspects of life. One watched over the harvest, another over health, one over love and sex, and so forth. The people believed that there was a great god who created everything, but then he sat back and just watched things develop.

When the Africans arrived in Cuba, they were divided up and sold, but they carried with them their religion. It was usually not quite the same as that of the other slaves they lived with, but it was similar. The slave owners, as good Catholics of their time, felt the need to convert the slaves to Christianity and so introduced them to their God and the saints. The slaves, with their pantheon of African deities already in place, accepted these new "deities"—the saints—into their beliefs. To blend the two spiritual traditions, the slaves linked the saints to the African deities with similar stories or powers. Hence, Saint Barbara became mixed with Changó, Saint Lazarus with Babalú Ayé, the Virgen de la Caridad del Cobre with Ochún, and so forth.

African religious practices were legalized in Cuba as of 1870. In 1880, when slavery was eliminated, one of the freed slaves, Eulogio Gutierrez, went back to Africa to learn more about his homeland. He eventually returned to Cuba as the first *babalao*.[6]

The high priests of Santeria are viewed as wise men, like shamans. They are who people look to for advice, direction, and solutions to their problems. One told me that, these days, *babalaos* need to be part psychiatrist because people bring them all of their problems. A *babalao* must have the abilities of an *espiritista*, that is, the ability to contact the spirit world. However, their abilities of divination are tapped through the *orishas* of Santeria. They might throw shells or coconut pieces to read for a consultation. If there is something a person desires, a *babalao* can advise him or her on what should be offered to the *orishas*.

Music and dancing are part of the ritual of Santeria. The rhythm of beating drums and songs in the Yoruba language call the *orishas* and set people to swaying and dancing. The rhythms and the ritual can bring on a trance-like mystical state. To become an initiate of Santeria, one must pass through a ceremony and become an *hijo de santo* (son of a saint). Whereas in Africa the *orishas* possessed their direct-blood descendants, in Cuba the connection is not one of direct descendancy, because families were broken up in the time of slavery. Instead, possession is of a spiritual child, who therefore is an *hijo de santo*. Initiates are noticeable on the streets of Havana because they are dressed all in white, including shoes and head covering.

Natalia Bolívar is the best authority on Santeria in Cuba. Trained in ethnography, she has written several books and has done extensive research on Afro-Cuban religions. Some call her the white goddess of the black gods. Natalia has short gray hair, fair skin, and eyes that reflect a profound intellect. Her commanding presence is one of wisdom and understanding. She is much in demand as a lecturer because of her deep knowledge of her subject and is sought after, as well, for her spiritual insights. I spent hours visiting with her in her apartment, which is filled with light, plants, and artwork. She has created an oasis around herself where politics are left behind. In her book *The Orishas of Cuba* she reveals in great detail the history and characteristics of the *orishas*. Her descriptions, as the following excerpts show, help to explain how Santeria works in the lives of Cubans.

Changó is the god of fire, of thunder, of war, of dance, of music, and of male beauty. . . . He represents many human virtues and imperfections. He is a hard worker, brave, a good friend, and a healer, but is also a liar, a womanizer, and quarrelsome. . . . His color is red, the color of blood and of love. . . . His syncretic counterpart is Saint Barbara.

Ochún is in charge of femininity and rivers. She is a symbol of flirtation, grace, and feminine sexuality. . . . She is represented as a beautiful mulatta who is kind, a good dancer, likes parties, and is always happy. She can also *resolver* everything. . . . Her color is yellow. . . . Her counterpart is the Virgen de la Caridad del Cobre.

Yemayá is the mother of life and is considered the mother of all the *orishas*. She holds dominion over the water and represents the sea, the fundamental source of life. . . . She likes to hunt and use a machete. She is indomitable and astute. Her color is blue and her counterpart is the Virgen de Regla.

Elegguá is the *orisha* which holds the keys to destiny and opens or closes the door to disgrace or happiness. He is the personification of chance and death. . . . His colors are red and black, representing life and death. . . . His syncretic counterpart can be Saint Anthony of Padua or the boy of Atocha [referring to a child who entered a prison in the time of the Moorish occupation of Spain and fed the prisoners. He fed countless prisoners, yet his baskets remained full.]

Obbatalá is the *orisha* which created the earth and sculpted the human being. This supremely pure deity is in charge of all that is white, the head, thoughts, and dreams. . . . Obbatalá is merciful and loves peace and harmony. . . . Obbatalá's color is white. . . .

The various forms may be syncretized with the Virgen de las Mercedes, Jesus of Nazareth, the Eye of Divine Providence, and even God Almighty.[7]

Followers of Santeria often wear beaded necklaces in the colors of their protectors, have altars in their homes, and ask the *orishas* for assistance. When a believer asks something of the gods, he or she will dedicate something to an *orisha*—herbs, flowers, or even a dead animal, such as a chicken. In Parque Lenin while I was horseback riding one Saturday morning, I asked my trainer about a strange large tree I saw. The tree, a *ceiba,* had a smooth light-colored trunk and limbs high above that looked like they could have been roots—as if the tree had been stuck into the ground upside down. That variety of tree, he told me, was important in Santeria. We rode over to the base of the tree and saw offerings that had been left—strips of red cloth for Changó, herbs, and pieces of fruit. Apparently, this tree was particularly desirable because it was far from the road, and believers could make their petitions in relative privacy.

The *orishas* help some people cope with the difficult paths their lives have taken. One young artist who mixes the theme of Santeria with images of *jineteras* said, "It is what I see. Girls who never believed in anything before are suddenly talking about Ochún and Yemayá. I think it makes it easier for them to deal with what they are doing." Considering that Ochún rules over femininity, it is not surprising that young women trying to earn a living by attracting men would look to her for support.

On September 8, the day of Cuba's patron saint, Caridad del Cobre, whose syncretic pairing is Ochún, I attended my friend Margarita's saint-day party. Her altar to Ochún/Caridad del Cobre had been decorated with sunflowers and candles and draped with sheer yellow and blue fabric. Two dolls were on the shelf below the Virgin. Margarita explained that one was a gypsy and another was an African woman; they represented her two strongest guardian spirits.

When the party began, there were a number of bottles of rum placed on the altar—gifts to Ochún—which were drunk as the party progressed. It was a lively party with salsa music, dancing, food, and drink that culminated in a special ceremony to honor Ochún.

Although Santeria is the most prominent tradition, there are others. The Sociedad Secreta Abakua, or the Secret Society of Abakua, may be the most organized. It is an all-male society that has its roots in a group of blacks from Cameroon and Southeast Nigeria who worked to raise money to free slaves. During colonial times, the crown tried to limit their access to the independence movement. In 1857, the first white Abakua group was formed. The Abakua follow a strong moral code, but their ceremony and liturgy are secret. To join the society, the Abakua require that one "be an adult male; be a good son, good father, good brother, good friend; be moral and respect others; not have a police record; not harbor vices; not commit acts which will dishonor the institution, neither in public nor in private; and be faithful to the power and not betray the secret."[8]

Although the Abakua fought in the war of independence from Spain and for Fidel, for years they were denied recognition by the State. This may be because this brotherhood is a force, and because it is secret, it would have remained out of the grasp of Fidel had it been "legalized." When an organization is not recognized, there is always the threat of punishment by the State for illegal association. One Abakua said in a discussion, "When I was in the Army, they kept pushing me, saying 'Are you Abakua? Are you Abakua?' We have done so much for this country, why do they not recognize us?"

Palo Monte, another variant, finds its roots in Bantu tribes of the Congo. Although it shares some deities with Santeria, they carry different names. This tradition has to do with the interrelationship between the spirits of ancestors and all of the vibrations of nature—from animals, waters, the earth, the trees, plants, and herbs. It has been handed down orally from the sixteenth century.[9]

Obbatalá, Changó, Yemayá, Ochún, and the other gods of Santeria are very much alive on the island. In a world where everything is beyond one's control, a *babalao*'s shared wisdom gives Cubans a greater clarity about their life and hope for their future. Believing has a tremendous power.

Notes

1 *Conferencia de Obispos Católicos de Cuba* letter, May 16, 1995, Havana.

2 *Vitral: Revista del Centro Católico de Formación Cívica y Religiosa de Pinar del Río,* May 1996.

3 Catherine L. Albanese, *America Religion and Religions* (Belmont, CA: Wadsworth Publishing, 1992), 250.

4 Natalia Bolívar Aróstegui, lecture on *espiritismo*, UNEAC, 1996.

5 Argelio Santiesteban, *El Habla Cubana Popular de Hoy* (Havana: Editorial de Ciencias Sociales, 1992), 47.

6 Natalia Bolívar Aróstegui, lecture on Regla de Ocha o Santeria, UNEAC, 1996.

7 Natalia Bolívar Aróstegui, *Los Orishas en Cuba* (Havana: Pm Ediciones, 1994).

8 Natalia Bolívar Aróstegui, lecture on Sociedad Secreta Abakua, UNEAC, 1996.

9 Natalia Bolívar Aróstegui, lecture on Reglas de Palo, UNEAC, 1996.

< 18 >

Caridad del Cobre

Si te vas al Cobre, no me traigas flores sino una piedrecita de la Caridad.
(If you go to Cobre, don't bring me flowers, but rather a little stone
from Caridad.)—lyric from a Cuban folk song

If there is a religious focal point in Cuba, it lies with the Virgen de
la Caridad del Cobre (Our Lady of Charity of Cobre), the patron
saint of Cuba. Common wisdom has it that in 1628, three fishermen were caught in a storm in the Gulf of Nipe and feared for their
lives. A mulatta madonna came to them on the water, dry on the
stormy sea. In her left arm she held the infant Jesus. In her right she
held a gold cross. On the wooden planks upon which she was floating were the words "I am the Virgen de la Caridad." After seeing
her and perceiving the event to be a miracle, the fishermen made it
safely home. They established a shrine to her in the nearest village,
Cobre, a town not far from Santiago de Cuba that is the site of a
copper mine. One historian has suggested that there may be another
explanation for Caridad's origin. It is possible that Caridad might
be related to Our Lady of Charity of Illescas, an ancient and mirac-
ulous madonna revered in sixteenth century Spain, who was vener-
ated in Cobre for at least twenty years before the fishermen set sail.[1]

Whether Caridad del Cobre is related to Our Lady of Illescas may
never be known. What is important is her power in Cuba. The Virgen de la Caridad is not only the patron saint of the island, she is also
the counterpart of Ochún. She is holy to followers of both the
Catholic faith and Santeria. She is believed to heal and to perform
miracles.

The drive to Cobre from Santiago leads up a scenic but narrow and winding road through a hilly landscape that is lush and green. The cream-colored church that was built for Caridad lies at the top of a rise. When a car pulls into the parking lot, its passengers are assailed by dozens of young black men and boys trying to sell small shiny stones they have taken from the nearby copper mine—the famous *piedrecitas* referred to in the Cuban folk song. The stones are supposed to be talismans for good luck. One of the young men will offer to take care of the car. Others will try to sell handicrafts.

Entering the church is like stepping into another world. The worries and troubles of life fall from the shoulders of the faithful as they cross into this haven of peace. It is a sacred place, consecrated by the millions of Cubans who have made pilgrimages there. It is a place of hope, a place to give thanks, a place to pray for miracles. In the entry hall there are displays of letters and photos of people who have been touched by the power of Caridad del Cobre. Among them are a letter from a mother whose child survived surgery and photographs of rafters who had made it to Guantanamo and hoped to reach the United States. There are also medals, athletes' trophies, and pieces of jewelry given in thanks for answered prayers. Cubans have precious little, yet they leave gifts at the shrine. These people believe that others have received response to prayer, and they believe their prayers will be heard as well. The shrine at Cobre is an outward manifestation of a tremendous and profound faith in God.

The Virgen de la Caridad, a fifteen-inch-tall wooden madonna draped in an elaborate cloth gown, is upstairs in the church, set protectively behind glass. From a perch above an altar decorated with flowers, in a quiet space with fewer than ten rows of pews, Caridad looks on those who pray. Here the faithful come, make their petitions, and give thanks. When mass is held in the large sanctuary below, the madonna is turned to face the congregation. The quiet stillness of the atmosphere is pregnant with the power of God.

At a party at my home the night before I left for Santiago de Cuba, a young Cuban man who knew I would be going to Cobre solemnly

asked me, "Please, pray for my daughters." A group nearby over-
heard, and one man, wanting to confirm my destination, asked,
"You will be going to Cobre?" When I responded that I would be seeing the Virgen de la Caridad del Cobre, he had a simple request:
"Pray for us." Then another person echoed his sentiment, saying,
"Pray for us. Pray for all of us Cubans. Caridad del Cobre listens—
and she works miracles."

I hope she was listening.

Note

1 Irene Wright, "Our Lady of Charity," *The Hispanic American Historical Review,* vol. 5, no. 4 (1922): 709–717.

Index

Abakua, Secret Society of the, 165,
170
Academics: exchanges of, 85–86;
political survival of, 17
Acanda, Jorge, 17
African deities, 165–166
African slaves, 165–166
Afro-Cuban music, 4, 148–149
Afro-Cuban religions, 155; tradi-
tions of, 165–171
Agricultural markets, 29–30
Agromercados. See Food, markets
for
Alarcon, Ricardo, 73, 114, 135
Albright, Madeleine, 132, 133
Alcoholism, 149
Alfonso, Miguel, 114, 123
Amagro, Lionel Morejon, 130, 136
America: automobiles of, 95–96;
baseball of, 94–95; Cuban policy
of, 85–91; Cubans' affinity for,
93–98; emigration to, 99–104;
ideas of, 14; imperialist, 13–14;
movies of, 96–97; music of,
93–94; products of, 95–97; as the
promised land, 98; radio stations
broadcasting from, 117–118; as
scapegoat, 135; table manners of,
97; threat of, 12–13
American Association of Publishers,
exhibit of, 17–18
Anthony of Padua, Saint, 168
Anti-American marches, 24

Arcos, Gustavo, 102, 126–127
Artists, 72–73
Association of Independent Econo-
mists, 125
Astudillo, Felix Pita, 86–87
Asylum seekers, 114
Atlanta Braves, 95
August exodus, 99–101
Aung San Suu Kyi, 81
Automobiles, 95–96

Babalaos. See Priest (Santeria)
Babalú Ayé, 166
Baguer, Nestor, 120–121
Baldriche, Pedro, 73
Balseros. See Rafters
Bantu tribes, religion of, 165,
170
Barbara, Saint, 166, 168
Baseball, 94–95
Basic necessities: scarcity of, 3,
25–26; supplied by State, 10
Batista, rebellion against, 81
Bay of Pigs, 12, 60–61
Beaches, 62
Black market, 33–34; building
materials on, 42; medicine on,
68
Blaha, Cob, 112, 149
Blake, Ron, 94
Bodeguita del Medio, 60
Bolívar, Natalia, 167–169
Bonne, Felix, 126n, 129

Books, supplied by U.S. Interests Section, 79–80, 90–91

Brothers to the Rescue flights, 131–135

Buildings, disrepair of, 41–42

Buro de Prensa Independiente, 123–124

Cable News Network (CNN), Castro interview on, 8

Cane-cutting brigades, 23

Canon firing reenactment, 62–63

Caridad del Cobre. See Virgen de la Caridad del Cobre

Caritas, 156

Castañeda, Jorge, 90

Castro, Fidel: in America, 99; baseball and, 95; Brothers to the Rescue aircraft incident and, 132–134; charisma of, 8; control of migration, 114; images of, 72–73; loyalty to, 7–24; nicknames for, 11; Pope's visit and, 161–162; speeches of, 8–9; on U.S. Track Two policy, 86

Castro, Raul, 14; on free press, 117; speech of at Fifth Party Plenum, 89, 137–140; supporting agricultural markets, 29–30

Catholic Center for Religious and Civic Formation, 160

Catholic Church, 3, 155, 156–162; as conscience of Cuba, 157–158; on equality, 157–158; in future of Cuba, 158–159; roots of, 156

Celebration, 149–151

Censorship, 118–119

Change, fear of, 81–83

Changó, 166, 175

Charter flights, from Miami, 40–41

Chaviano, Francisco, 100

Children: malnourished, 28; as prostitutes, 50–51

Christian religions, 3, 155–162. See also Catholic Church; Protestants

Christmas trees, debate on, 161

Cienfuegos, Camilo, 82

Civic groups, 77–80; forming of, 75–76; before Revolution, 75

Civics classes, 160

Clinton, Bill: Helms-Burton legislation and, 131–132; relaxed travel restrictions by, 39–40

Cobre, 173–174

Coffee rations, 27

Coleman, Steve, 94

Committee for the Defense of the Revolution, 10–11

Communication, creativity in, 11

Communism. See Revolution; State

Communist groups, 75

Communist Party: faithful of, 14–15; officials, fall from grace of, 17–18

Community: sense of, 4, 145–147; spirit of, 147–148, 149–151, 153

Concilio Cubano, 125–136, 129–130; crackdown on, 121–122; diverting attention from, 134–136

Conference of Catholic Bishops, 157–158

Conrado, Padre Jose, 159–160

Conspicuous consumption, 51–53

Copacabana, 49

Counterrevolutionary, 23

Cuban Adjustment Act, 128
Cuban Association of Independent
    Journalists (APIC), 120–121
Cuban Book Institute, 18
Cuban Committee for Human
    Rights, 126–127
Cuban Democracy Act, 85–86
Cuban identity, pride in, 145–151
Cuban Interests Section, restriction
    of, 131–132
Cuban jazz festival, 93–94
Cuban MiG fighters, shooting down
    civilian airplanes, 130–135,
    133–136
Cubans, spirit of, 145–151
Cuban Union of Writers and Artists,
    97
Cuban-U.S. relations. *See* U.S.-
    Cuban relations
CubaPress, 119–120, 123, 124
Cuenta propia. See Self-employment
Cultural exchanges, 85–86

Daily life, 25–34
Dale, J. D., 107
Dancing, 149
Dangerousness, 20
Dausa, Rafael, 91
Departure, illegal, 100
Desacato. See Irreverence
Diplomatic missions, 43
Diplomats, dangerous ideas of, 138
Diplomat's store, 32–33
Diplotienda. See Diplomat's store
Disillusionment, 23–24
Disrespect. *See* Irreverence
Dissidents, 16; charges against, 21;
    crackdown on, 135–136; legal

migration of, 103–104. *See also*
    Opposition groups
Doble moral. See Dual morality
Doctors, numbers of, 65
Dollar grocery stores, 33
Dollars: from family members
    abroad, 39–40; permission to
    hold, 29; working for, 41–44
Dual morality, 16–17, 22, 24, 126

Economic groups, 35
Economy: embargo and, 13, 85;
    growth of, 52–53; private produc-
    tion in, 30; scarcities and, 25–28;
    during Special Period, 28–29;
    troubles of, 3, 41–42, 102, 145;
    widening gap between rich and
    poor in, 52–53. *See also* Dollars;
    Markets; Salaries
Education, 3, 71–73
Elegguá, 168
Embargo, U.S., 13, 85
Emigration, 99–104
Employment. *See* Dollars; Peso
    salaries; Self-employment
Enemy propaganda, 20, 21–22
English, command of, 43–44
Environmental groups, 76
Espin, Wilma, 51
Espiritismo. See Mysticism; Spiritual-
    ism
Evangelical churches, 160
Evil eye, 163–164

Family relationships, 146–148
Farmers: attack on, 138–139; small,
    30
Federation of Cuban Women, 51, 75

Federation of University Students, 75
Food: black market for, 33–34; in *diplotienda,* 32–33; easing shortages of, 29–30; markets for, 29–30; scarcity of, 25–28, 32–33; as social event, 149–150; for tourists, 56
Foreign firms, 42–43
Foreign investments, 43
Fox family, 162–163
Freedom of press, 120
Free expression, lack of, 71–72
Friendship, reliance on, 145–148

Garcia, Jose Rivero, 123
God, faith in, 154–155
Gonzalez, Celina, 4, 150
Gonzalez, Georgina, 129
Gonzalez, Orlando, 78, 80
Gore, Al, 90
Government. *See* State
Grand Masonic Lodge, 76, 77–78
Granma (newspaper), 21, 117; anti-American harangues in, 85–87; news coverage in, 118–119
Gras, Miriam, 72
Grupusculos, 128
Guajira music, 4, 150
"Guantanamera," 150
Guantanamo: cultural center at, 90; markets in, 30–31; rafter camps in, 105–107
Guevara, Che, 82
Gusano. See Counterrevolutionary
Gutierrez, Eulogio, 166

Habana Press, 122
Hand gestures, as communication, 11

Handicrafts, 59
Hargrove, Roy, 94
Hart, Armando, 18
Havana: decaying infrastructure of, 2; economy of, 32–33, 99–100; entertainment in, 58–59; markets in, 29–30
Havana Vieja cathedral, 156
Health care: access to, 66–67; infectious disease and, 66; lack of medicine in, 67–68; renown of, 65–66; sanitation and, 69–71
Helms, Jesse, 13
Helms-Burton legislation, 132–133; Cuban response to, 137–140
Henley, William Ernest, 125
Hijacking incident, 114
Homemade wares, 45
Hope, loss of, 100–102
Hospitals, 66; transportation to, 66–67
"Hotel California," 101
Hotel Nacional, 57–58
Hotel Riviera, Palacio de la Salsa, 50, 58
Hotels: prostitutes in, 55–56, 57–58; service in, 56–57
Human rights, 90–91, 134; groups, 126–127; information about, 126–127
Human spirit, 145–151

Illescas, Our Lady of, 173
Immigrant visas, lottery for, 109–111
Independent thinkers, 88–89
Individualism, attack on, 139
Infant mortality rate, 65

Infections, prevalence of, 66
Information flow, 85, 89–91; news media and, 117–124
Infrastructure, disintegrating, 2
Intellectual integrity, 72
Intellectuals: attack on, 137–140; opportunities for, 87; in Track Two program, 88–89
International news, 117
Internet, independent journalists on, 119–120
Invasion, threat of, 12–13
Irreverence, 20, 21

Jazz, Cuban and American exchange of, 93–94
Jineteras. See Prostitution
Joint-venture firms, 42–43
Journalists, independent, 119–124

Kardec, Alan, 163

Lage, Carlos, 73, 137
Lam, Galeria Wilfredo, 60
Langley, Lester, 90
Language, spoken, 11
Lazarus, Saint, 166
Legal migration, encouragement of, 106–107
Lenin Monument, 2
Leon, Gloria, 88
Leptospirosis, 69–70
Libraries, 79–80, 90
Life, joy of, 149–151
Lillian Hellman Foundation, 123
Literacy rate, 65
Lopez, Cesar, 94
Lottery, 109–111

Maceo, Antonio, 77
Mala vista. See Evil eye
Malecón, fair on, 59
Malnutrition, 28
Manzano, Rene Gomez, 126n
Mao Zedong, 83
Markets, 29–33; food, 29–30; outside Havana, 30–33
Marrero, Lucrecia, 77, 78–79, 80
Marriage, as socialist love, 10
Martí, José, 77; in America, 99; nationalism of, 145; writings of, 91
Martinez, Julio, 122
Masonic library, 79–80
Masons, 19–20, 75, 76–80
Matanzas market, 31–32
May Day celebrations, 24
Medical research teams, 65
Medicine, scarcity of, 67–68
Melia Cohiba, 57
Menocal, Padre Manuel H. de Cespedes Garcia, 158–159
Mexican National Day celebration, 8
Miami: charter flights from, 40–41; "mafiosos" of, 13, 83; money flowing to Cuba from, 39–40; "terrorist organizations" of, 128
Miami Herald (newspaper), 21, 119, 120, 121
Migration, 99–104; as treason, 102–104; of youth, 101–103. *See also* Rafters
Migration accords, 105–115; excludables from, 106–107; lottery under, 109–111; upholding of, 111–114
Military service, compulsory, 12–13

Mistrust, as barrier to rebellion, 81–82
Moncada barracks attack, 86
El Morro fortress, 63
Movies, American, 96–97
Museo de la Revolución, 60
Music, 58, 150; Afro-Cuban, 148–149; Cuban and American exchange of, 93–94; Guajira, 150
Mysticism, 153, 154, 162–171. *See also* Spirituality
Mystics, advice from, 164–165

Neighborhoods, 148
Netherlands, radio stations broadcasting from, 117–118
News media: control of, 117–124; covering Brothers to the Rescue incident, 133; deciphering messages of, 137–138
Newspapers, 118–119; State control of, 17
Noel, Cecilia, 94
Nogueras, Olance, 122–123
Nongovernmental organizations, 76–80
Nostalgia, for pre-Revolutionary times, 141–142
El Nuevo Herald (newspaper), 21, 119
Nutritional problems, 68–69

Obbatalá, 168–169
Ochún, 166, 169–171
O'Connor, Ted, 107, 108
Opposition groups, 125–136; discrediting, 128–129; diverting attention from, 134–136; people

attracted to, 126–127; risks of joining, 127–128; umbrella organization for, 129–130
Orishas, 167–169
Ortega, Cardinal Jaime, 82, 157
Orwell, George, 90
Ostracism, 89

Paladares. See Restaurants, private
Palo Monte, 165, 170
Pardo, Gustavo, 79
Party Plenum, 136; fifth, 14, 137–140
Peligrosidad. See Dangerousness
Pelletier, Yanez, 129
Pensions, 27
Peso salaries, 35–39
Pharmacies, dollar, 67–68
Piñeda, Alfonso, 107
Playa Giron. *See* Bay of Pigs
Plaza de la Catedral, 59–60
Political categories, 14–17
Political crimes, 20–22
Political survival, 16–17
Pope John Paul II, visit by, 161–162
Press: independent, 119–124; State control of, 117–119
Priest (Catholic), role of, 157–160
Priest (Santeria): spiritual power of, 166, 167; wisdom of, 171
Prieto, Abel, 97
Print media, State control of, 117
Private enterprise, under Special Period, 29
Propaganda, 118–119; with Brothers to the Rescue incident, 133; enemy, 20, 21–22
Propaganda enemiga. See Enemy propaganda

Prostitution, 48–51; in tourist hotels, 55–56, 57–58
Protestants, 155, 160–162
Pupo, Lt. Col. Jose Fernandez, 114

Radio Martí, 101, 117–118, 119–120, 121, 124
Radio Rebelde, 21, 121
Radio stations: foreign, 72; international, 117–118; State control of, 117
Rafter crisis, 105, 146
Rafters, 99, 100–102; returned to Cuba, 105–109, 112–114
Ration cards, 33
Rats, 69–70
Rebellion, barriers to, 81–84
Refugee status, 103
Regla de Ocha. *See* Santeria
Reich, Robert, 90
Religious faith, 153–171, 174–175. *See also* Mysticism; Spiritualism; Spirituality; *specific religions*
Reno, Attorney Gen. Janet, 105
Reporters Without Borders, 120, 123
Resolver. See Solutions, finding
Responsibility, sense of, 146
Restano, Yndamiro, 120, 123
Restaurants, private, 46–47; taxes on, 47
Revolution: disillusionment with, 23–24; disrespect for, 20, 21; loyalty to, 7–24; static, 83; triumphs of, 3, 65–73
Rich, newly, 51–53
Rivero, Raul, 123
Robaina, Roberto, 132, 133

Roque, Marta Beatriz, 53, 70, 125–126, 128, 136

Salaries: of educated people, 27; peso, 35–39
Salida ilegal. See Departure, illegal
Salmon, Sandra, 107, 108
Salsa music, 58
Sanchez, Elizardo, 130
Sanitary conditions, deteriorating, 69–71
Santeria, 155, 160, 165–171
Sea, contemplation of, 154
Self-censorship, 73
Self-employed, attack on, 138–139
Self-employment, 44–47
Sex tourism, 48
Shaw, Bernard, 8
Slaves, religions of, 165–171
Socialist utopia, 2
Sociedad Secreta Abakua, 165, 170
Solano, Rafael, 103, 121–122
Solutions, finding, 35–40, 104
Soviet aid, 2, 28; end of, 137
Spain: colonialism of, 156; radio stations broadcasting from, 117–118
Special Period, 11, 25–26; declaration of, 28–29; health care deterioration during, 65
Spiritualism, 3, 155, 162–165; modern beginning of, 162–163
Spirituality, 3, 153–171. *See also* Mysticism
State: bureaucracy of, 9–10; employees of, 35–39; employment agency of, 43; food rationing by, 26–28; opposition to, 125–136; organizations of, 75; power of,

State (*cont.*)
   18–20; religion and, 160–162;
   theft from warehouses of, 33–34.
   See also Revolution; State Security
State Security: apparatus of, 10–12;
   infiltrating opposition groups,
   128–129; pervasive presence of,
   81
Sugarcane workers, 38–39
Surveillance, 12
Survival: focus on, 83–84; religious
   faith and, 154–155

Television, State control of, 117
Terry, Yosvany, 94
13 de Marzo, sinking of, 99–100
Thought, freedom of, 71–72
Toirac, Jose Angel, 72–73
Torricelli, Sen. Robert, 85
Tourism: jobs in, 41, 42, 43; pro-
   motion of, 48
Tourist attractions, 57–60
Tourists: dangerous ideas of, 138;
   life for, 55–64; prostitutes and,
   55–56, 57–58
Trabajadores (newspaper), 122
Track Two policy, 85–91
Travel restrictions, relaxing of,
   39–40
Tropicana, floor show at, 58–59

Unemployed, voluntarily, 15–16
Union of Young Communists, 24,
   75
United States. *See* America; U.S.-
   Cuban relations
Universal Declaration of Human
   Rights, 126–127, 134

Universities, 90
University of Havana, books supplied to, 90
U.S.-Cuban relations, 85–91; after
   migration accords, 111–114; with
   Brothers to the Rescue incident,
   131–136; migration accords and,
   105–109; before Revolution, 93
U.S. Interests Section: books and
   pamphlets supplied by, 79–80,
   90–91; contact with, 14; danger
   of contact with, 87–88; Masons
   and, 19–20; monitoring return of
   rafters, 112–114
USIS art exhibit, 77–79

Valdés, Chucho, 94
Valdés, Dagoberto, 160
Valdivia, Roxana, 21–22
Varadero, tourism in, 55
Vega, Jesús, 88–89
Veloz, Ramon Fabian, 150
Viaggiare, 48
Virgen de la Caridad del Cobre,
   166, 168, 169, 173–175
Virgen de las Mercedes, 169
Virgen de Regla, 168
Vitral (magazine), 158–159, 160

War veterans, lack of provisions for,
   36
Water supply, impurities in, 37
World Series, 94–95

Yemayá, 168
Yoruba slaves, 165
Young Pioneers, 75
Youth, leaving Cuba, 101–103

Latin American Silhouettes
Studies in History and Culture

William H. Beezley and
Judith Ewell
Editors

Volumes Published

Silvia Marina Arrom and Servando Ortoll, eds., *Riots in the Cities: Popular Politics and the Urban Poor in Latin America, 1765–1910* (1996). Cloth ISBN 0-8420-2580-4 Paper ISBN 0-8420-2581-2

Roderic Ai Camp, ed., *Polling for Democracy: Public Opinion and Political Liberalization in Mexico* (1996). ISBN 0-8420-2583-9

Brian Loveman and Thomas M. Davies, Jr., eds., *The Politics of Antipolitics: The Military in Latin America*, 3d ed., revised and updated (1996). Cloth ISBN 0-8420-2609-6 Paper ISBN 0-8420-2611-8

Joseph S. Tulchin, Andrés Serbín, and Rafael Hernández, eds., *Cuba and the Caribbean: Regional Issues and Trends in the Post-Cold War Era* (1997). ISBN 0-8420-2652-5

Thomas W. Walker, ed., *Nicaragua without Illusions: Regime Transition and Structural Adjustment in the 1990s* (1997). Cloth ISBN 0-8420-2578-2 Paper ISBN 0-8420-2579-0

Dianne Walta Hart, *Undocumented in L.A.: An Immigrant's Story* (1997). Cloth ISBN 0-8420-2648-7 Paper ISBN 0-8420-2649-5

Jaime E. Rodríguez O. and Kathryn Vincent, eds., *Myths, Misdeeds, and Misunderstandings: The Roots of Conflict in U.S.-Mexican Relations* (1997). ISBN 0-8420-2662-2

Jaime E. Rodríguez O. and Kathryn Vincent, eds., *Common Border, Uncommon Paths: Race, Culture, and National Identity in U.S.-Mexican Relations* (1997). ISBN 0-8420-2673-8

William H. Beezley and Judith Ewell, eds., *The Human Tradition in Modern Latin America* (1997). Cloth ISBN 0-8420-2612-6 Paper ISBN 0-8420-2613-4

Donald F. Stevens, ed., *Based on a True Story:Latin American History at the Movies* (1997). Cloth ISBN 0-8420-2582-0 Paper ISBN 0-8420-2781-5

Jaime E. Rodríguez O., ed., *The Origins of Mexican National Politics, 1808–1847* (1997). Paper ISBN 0-8420-2723-8

Che Guevara, *Guerrilla Warfare*, with revised and updated introduction and case studies by Brian Loveman and Thomas M. Davies, Jr., 3d ed. (1997). Cloth ISBN 0-8420-2677-0 Paper ISBN 0-8420-2678-9

Adrian A. Bantjes, *As If Jesus Walked on Earth: Cardenismo, Sonora, and the Mexican Revolution* (1998). ISBN 0-8420-2653-3

Henry A. Dietz and Gil Shidlo, eds., *Urban Elections in Democratic Latin America* (1998). Cloth ISBN 0-8420-2627-4 Paper ISBN 0-8420-2628-2

A. Kim Clark, *The Redemptive Work: Railway and Nation in Ecuador, 1895–1930* (1998). ISBN 0-8420 2674-6

Joseph S. Tulchin, ed., with Allison M. Garland, *Argentina: The Challenges of Modernization* (1998). ISBN 0-8420-2721-1

Louis A. Pérez, Jr., ed., *Impressions of Cuba in the Nineteenth Century: The*

Travel Diary of Joseph J. Dimock (1998). Cloth ISBN 0-8420-2657-6 Paper ISBN 0-8420-2658-4

June E. Hahner, ed., *Women through Women's Eyes: Latin American Women in Nineteenth-Century Travel Accounts* (1998). Cloth ISBN 0-8420-2633-9 Paper ISBN 0-8420-2634-7

James P. Brennan, ed., *Peronism and Argentina* (1998). ISBN 0-8420-2706-8

John Mason Hart, ed., *Border Crossings: Mexican and Mexican-American Workers* (1998). Cloth ISBN 0-8420-2716-5 Paper ISBN 0-8420-2717-3

Brian Loveman, *For* la Patria: *Politics and the Armed Forces in Latin America* (1999). Cloth ISBN 0-8420-2772-6 Paper ISBN 0-8420-2773-4

Guy P. C. Thomson, with David G. LaFrance, *Patriotism, Politics, and Popular Liberalism in Nineteenth-Century Mexico: Juan Francisco Lucas and the Puebla Sierra* (1999). ISBN 0-8420-2683-5

Robert Woodmansee Herr, in collaboration with Richard Herr, *An American Family in the Mexican Revolution* (1999). ISBN 0-8420-2724-6

Juan Pedro Viqueira Albán, trans. Sonya Lipsett-Rivera and Sergio Rivera Ayala, *Propriety and Permissiveness in Bourbon Mexico* (1999).

Cloth ISBN 0-8420-2466-2 Paper ISBN 0-8420-2467-0

Stephen R. Niblo, *Mexico in the 1940s: Modernity, Politics, and Corruption* (1999). ISBN 0-8420-2794-7

David E. Lorey, *The U.S.-Mexican Border in the Twentieth Century* (1999). Cloth ISBN 0-8420-2755-6 Paper ISBN 0-8420-2756-4

Joanne Hershfield and David R. Maciel, eds., *Mexico's Cinema: A Century of Films and Filmmakers* (2000). Cloth ISBN 0-8420-2681-9 Paper ISBN 0-8420-2682-7

Peter V. N. Henderson, *In the Absence of Don Porfirio: Francisco León de la Barra and the Mexican Revolution* (2000). ISBN 0-8420-2774-2

Mark T. Gilderhus, *The Second Century: U.S.-Latin American Relations since 1889* (2000). Cloth ISBN 0-8420-2413-1 Paper ISBN 0-8420-2414-X

Catherine Moses, *Real Life in Castro's Cuba* (2000). Cloth ISBN 0-8420-2836-6 Paper ISBN 0-8420-2837-4

K. Lynn Stoner, ed./comp., with Luis Hipólito Serrano Pérez, *Cuban and Cuban-American Women: An Annotated Bibliography* (2000). ISBN 0-8420-2643-6

Thomas D. Schoonover, *The French in Central America: Culture and Commerce, 1820–1930* (2000). ISBN 0-8420-2792-0

ISBN 0-8420-2836-6

9 780842 028363